The Oregonian

VOL. XCVII— NO. 30,214

PORTLAND, OREGON, TUESDAY, SEPTEMBER 8, 1987

PRICE FIVE CENTS

Hey, Kids--Here's Elvis

New York Times

THE NEW YORK TIMES, SUNDAY, JUNE 18, 1972

'Prince From Another Planet'

He tried to settle the crowd down. "All right, friends, I'm gonna be here a few minutes," but the catcalls and boos were building, along with shouts of "We want Elvis," and the comic shared his self-pity with the audience. "You are 20,000, I am one, that's pretty rough odds."

Nobody cared. They howled until he gave up. "You win," he said, quitting the stage.

The MC appeared again, and told us we were going to have an intermission. Intermission from what? By now, we were growing restless. I said I felt sorry for the comic, and the girl who'd loved Elvis since she was 13

He was wrong.

At 9:15, Elvis appeared, materialized, in a white suit of lights, shining with golden appliqués, the shirt front slashed to show his chest. Around his shoulders was a cape lined in cloth of gold, its collar faced with scarlet. It was anything you wanted to call it, gaudy, vulgar, magnificent. He looked like a prince from another planet, narrow-eyed, with high Indian cheekbones and a smooth brown skin untouched by his 37 years. He was girdled by a great golden belt, a present from the International Hotel in Las Vegas for breaking all attendance records ("I wear it

turned, he moved, and when a girl threw a handkerchief on the stage, he wiped his forehead with it and threw it back, a gift of sweat from an earthy god.

The music was mixed, old rock with new, he did "Bridge Over Troubled Waters," and the ballad where the fellow asks the girl to lay her warm and tender body next to his, but it was when he'd get to one of the old Elvis numbers, "It's All Right, Mama," or "Love Me Tender," that the Garden came unglued. Young girls moaned, and stood in their seats trying to dance, and one kid took a giant leap from a loge seat clear to the stage, only to be caught (by some of that army which protects Elvis from his lovers) and taken away before she could come too close to her heart's desire. You had to hope she hadn't bruised a leg in that

Elvis Presley at Madison Square Garden
"Time stopped, and everyone was 17 again"

The New York Times/Larry Morris

Presley Show Brings In $

Elvis Presley's show played before 4,800 wildly enthusiastic persons at Bloch Arena last night and took in more than $52,000 for the USS Arizona Memorial Fund.

It even topped the $50,000 goal the rock 'n' roll star had set his sights on.

IT WAS a crackerjack show, a sellout, and the biggest single gate in the history of show business in Hawaii.

H. Tucker Gratz, chairman of the Pacific War Memorial Commission, said: "This occasion is a dream come true after 15 years. Tonight is the most important event in this effort.

Almost . . . "This all started when those daughter George Chaplin of The own teen-age

Tom Parker, Presley's manager) called George Chaplin and said: 'I know a young man whose services can be a big help.' "

GRATZ SAID that Parker came to Hawaii and set up the show and stipulated that every cent would go toward the War Memorial fund. "Forty-eight hours ago we met in this very room and we were $10,000 short," said Gratz. We made an agreement with Parker that he and Elvis would raise $5,000 if the War Memorial Commission would raise the other $5,000.

"I can assure you that on Dec. 7 of this year there will be a memorial."

The show was fast-paced and slick. It jumped. When Elvis came on the teenagers screamed for 2½ minutes without let-up, Elvis was

shirt and a blue string tie.

HE WIGGLES as much as he ever did. The Army didn't make him a bit conservative.

He started singing "Lone-

plause was like a shock wave.

Then "Buttercup" . . . the "Fools Such as I" . . . "Surrender" . . . "big three" . . . "Don't Be Cruel," and, of course, "Houn' Dog." The applause came roaring in.

A Gal Is Overcome By

THE FIRST ACT was Ph Ingall's orchestra, a brass combo that the audien lapped up. Soon the au ence clapped along in ti to the music.

Then Sterling Moss and his group perfor

thought my sorrow—pure
own teen-age

The King on the Road

ST.
MARTIN'S
PRESS

IN PERSON - ON THE STAGE - TH

ELVIS PRESLEY - TV & RECORDING STA

ELVIS PRESLEY AND H

ON THE SCREEN - TONY CU

ON THE STAGE
4:30 · 7:18 · 10:06
IN PERSON
ELVIS PRESLEY
STAGE SHOW

WEDNESDAY
THURSDAY
ELVIS
Presley
STAGE SHOW
3 Shows Daily

Editor: Mike Evans
Production Controller: Candida Lane
Picture Research: Liz Fowler
Art Director: Keith Martin
Art Editor: Valerie Hawthorn
Design: Atelier Design, Heinzight

Produced by Mandarin Offset
Printed in Hong Kong

Library of Congress Cataloging-in-Publication Data
available upon request
ISBN 0-312-14146-7

Simultaneously published in the United Kingdom
by Hamlyn, an imprint of Reed Consumer Books
Ltd.

Contents

A warm breeze, the scent of magnolia, the sound
of traffic passing in the distance. Someone's mother
calls a boy to dinner. This is how the song goes,
boasts one, and the others laugh as his fingers get
lost on the guitar neck. L-L-Let me see that thing.

A gust of wind, the sudden movement of a rainbow
on a clothesline. They giggle at the way he shakes.
I seen that on my uncle's farm, drawls another,
and they all demand that he do it again.

The smell of fried onions, the distant drone
of a newfangled television. A time of change.

The Hillbilly Cat

A hand reaches up to touch the performer, clearly beyond reach. Another hand and then another and again, a room full of reaching, of yearning, of souls uniting behind a knock-kneed fella wearing shocking chartreuse who would never pretend to understand how or why it all happened, would never lose his appreciation for the fact that it did, who remained polite and modest even when he could call the world his own.

Elvis Presley had never played professionally when Sun Records released his first 78 RPM single, 'That's All Right' on July 19, 1954. Within a month, the kid got his first taste of the spotlight at a rowdy Memphis roadhouse, and the record appeared on Billboard's regional country and western charts. Six more weeks and he debuted nationally on the *Grand Ole Opry*. Eighteen days later, he became a regular on the popular Saturday radio broadcast, the *Louisiana Hayride*. The Hayride reached throughout the South and into the Southwest, and Elvis, bassist Bill Black and guitarist Scotty Moore spent the next six months

putting three hundred thousand miles on Scotty's Chevrolet, satisfying the demands of a steady-building fan base. In May of 1955, in Jacksonville, Florida, Elvis fans exploded into the first of what became routine riots. In November, Sun Records sold his contract for a record-breaking price. Eighteen months after his first professional performance, he made his network TV premiere. Elvis Presley was about to turn twenty-one.

A New Song

Sing unto the Lord a new song. Praise Him with loud-sounding cymbals. Praise Him with clanging cymbals.

When Elvis was still driving a truck around Memphis – a job he held briefly with the Crown Electric company – the atom bomb cast a long shadow. Post-war America, awed by this capacity for destruction, sought the straight and narrow, hiding their doubts in a willful innocence. In the mushrooming darkness, anxiety crept like a virus. Paranoia, fed by McCarthyism, ran deep.

Stepping from darkness to light in the summer of 1954, Elvis Presley was a spectacle to behold. The thrust of his act was child's play a decade later, when society was won over by the hula hoop. But in the fifties, such gyrating was well hidden, consigned to burlesque and clubs on the seamier side of town. When his wiggle was beamed into dens of innocence via the new fangled television, the church-raised Christian was oft mistook for an instrument of Beelzebub. Singing that new song, banging that loud cymbal, it was completely alien. His records put racial questions splat in the listeners' faces, while his stage act forced issues of sex from back rooms to front pages. And the soundtrack to the debate was rock and roll.

Elvis' musical career began as show and tell. His Assembly of God church had a lot of audience participation, and he heard contemporary songs on the radio. He made his public debut as a fifth-grader, ten years old, October 3rd, 1945. It was Children's Day at the annual Mississippi-Alabama Fair and Dairy Show at the Tupelo fairgrounds.

That early publicity shot reveals the confusion.
These accidental hepsters are packaged as cowpokes.
There they are, the trio in western shirts grinning big
because they've got a secret up their sleeve.

1954-55 The Hillbilly Cat

Local radio station WELO sponsored a children's talent contest, and the usually shy boy had to stand on a chair to reach the microphone into which he sang 'Old Shep.'

In seventh grade, Elvis began taking his guitar to school. He would sing country or gospel songs, sometimes joined by a classmate, for anyone who wanted to listen. The Presleys moved to Memphis in November 1948, settling into the government-subsidized Lauderdale Courts a year later. Now Elvis and his instrument were no longer constant companions, but he continued to play at home, sometimes for friends, and after a couple years, watching kids in the housing projects gather beneath the magnolia tree and sing, he mustered the courage to bring his child's guitar and join in. His musicianship was based on instinct, augmented by his uncle Vester's informal advice and the occasional lessons from an older boy.

During his high school years, he mastered a small repertoire and could stumble through a few other songs. Recording 'My Happiness' for his mother at Sam Phillips's Memphis Recording Service fit perfectly his earnestness.

When Phillips called him back to test his voice on a ballad, Elvis' inexperience thwarted their attempts. Rehearsing with accompaniment proved not much better. Only when Elvis fought the mama's boy side of himself and tapped into his emerging prankster did he capture Mr. Phillips's attention and carry Scotty Moore and Bill Black through a door to a new world of sound.

Breakthrough

That breakthrough came on July 5, 1954. A blues number, Arthur Crudup's 'That's All Right.' Sam Phillips arranged for it to air on the radio three evenings later. The song was crazy enough for only one disc jockey, the original color-blind music appreciator himself – Dewey Phillips – who immediately embraced it. (They shared a last name, but not blood.) The audience response, the radio interview, and Dewey's enthusiasm encouraged the trio, and the next night they got a topsy-turvy take on Bill Monroe's bluegrass number 'Blue Moon of Kentucky.' Their unusual interpretations of these songs went to Mars when they were coupled, a distinctly 'black' song and a 'white' song, each given a treatment that made it unclear what sort of music they were creating.

The record was taken to be pressed. It had been a long time since 'Old Shep' at the fairgrounds, since magnolia trees, from 'My Happiness' to this punk take on what was known to be good and Christian. The craziness of these songs made people think, question their notions of 'black' and 'white' and, hell – their notions of good music. Even more, these songs made people move, made their heads bounce like puppies in a display window, their bodies shimmy with abandon.

Time to hit the stage, boy! Time to overcome reticence, to surmount those dreams of being a crooner like your heroes. Time to stand up in front of people, announce this music as just the first of many ideas. And they ain't even see you move yet. It's time to show'em you can mooove!

Saturday, July 17, marked the professional debut of Sun recording artist Elvis Presley. Scotty and Bill, while making history with Elvis, were also playing a regular weekend gig. The Starlite Wranglers were a country swing band, and their jazzy feel made them easy to dance to – therefore popular. With Elvis exhibiting such talent, there was talk of making him a, gosh, regular part of the Wranglers' show.

The Bon Air Club was on Highway 70, the outskirts of town, rural, walking distance to cotton fields. Its clientele was tough, and on Saturday nights they were as friendly with Jack Daniels and Jim Beam as they were with Jesus on Sunday. Step outside and say that, mah frien'.

The steel guitar whined, the fiddle hemmed and hawed, and the Wranglers began injecting a good time into their crowd. They wore matching outfits, they told a few jokes, and they had a good time on stage, all of which kept the crowd smiling, dancing, and drinking. When their first set ended, there was a little confusion about the new kid.

Gone was the rodeo costume he'd earlier masqueraded in. There was no more pretending he was something he was not, and Elvis came out in the cool clothes that he had seen on the avenue of black Memphis culture, Beale Street.

Elvis with the local Memphis D.J., Dewey Phillips

1954-55 The Hillbilly Cat

Scotty Moore, who was now managing him, had to get a little stern when he insisted that only he and Bill return on stage with the intermission act.

Murder

When Elvis took the stage, a murmur went through the crowd. This youngster with greasy hair and sideburns, the funny-fitting clothes, wasn't part of the usual act, and the unexpected made this audience uneasy. Bassist Bill Black thrilled to the tension that began creeping across the stage. He looked over at Scotty, who was grinning nervously as he anticipated the crowd's reaction to something they'd never heard, and then he looked at Elvis. It was time to start, but Elvis was short of breath. He turned to Scotty, then Bill, who grinned back widely. That put him at ease, and then he performed the only two songs his trio knew.

It wasn't that the crowd responded poorly, but Elvis was already anticipating the riots that were soon to greet him. When they applauded after the first song, then again after the second, and though they moved their heads in time to the beat, and though some danced and several seemed immensely pleased – Elvis, when they didn't react wildly, felt like he'd failed.

What he came to realize was how much he'd learned in just one night. When he returned the next week he was looser, more the prankster, and the fact that he was clearly starting to enjoy himself on stage allowed the audience to enjoy him more. When this performance was done, some even whooped, and in a place like the Bon Air, there was no higher sign of adulation. He quickly thanked Scotty and Bill, agreed to talk with them the next day because they had to get right back out on stage with the Wranglers, and with his head feeling a little light, he found the front door and drove home a few inches off the ground. He forgot his jacket and, too wired to be tired, returned. Inside, a few patrons recognized him and began to shout. Others turned and saw who it was, applause began to ripple through the club, and as if it was happening to someone else, Elvis found himself back on stage for a command performance. Delighted and more than a little dazed, he said something corny, stuttering a bit in his shy way, and the audience hooted because, having seen him a time or two already, he was still different but now they could relate to him. One-two-three-four, and the trio cranked it up, whipping through those same two songs and thinking sooner or later they'd better learn another one.

Earthquake

The record was released on July 19, the Monday between Bon Air gigs. The crowd response and the record's reception earned Elvis a slot just before the headliner. Scotty and Bill may have been used to performing, but never in an open-air venue like the Overton Park Band Shell. The stage was as big as some of the clubs they played, and they were nervous. If they had the jitters, Elvis was an earthquake. But when the time came, they took their place, waited for Elvis to strike that first chord, and then tore into their thing.

When Elvis Presley took the stage, it was like the Marines taking Normandy.

Greasy hair and funny-fitting clothes

1954-55 The Hillbilly Cat

When Elvis began swinging his whole body into the music – giving the audience a brand new image for their brand new soundtrack – they roared with approval. Bill began his own dance, a clownish version of Elvis' movements. Scotty dipped his head and looked at the floor and grinned, keeping the rhythm with his foot.

Hoopla

When Scotty began to book dates, the Wranglers took affront, and the trio moved from the Bon Air to the Eagle's Nest, another highway joint. The club was in a complex that also featured a swimming pool and a teen hangout, and when the kids heard Elvis start they'd rush the show, gladly being kicked out when the house band began. The trio played church rec rooms and social halls. They played to people on stretchers and in wheelchairs at the Kennedy Veterans Hospital. By early September, enough hoopla surrounded Elvis that he was billed to draw a crowd to the opening of a new shopping center.

When the record began receiving national attention, Sam Phillips contacted the *Grand Ole Opry*, whose radio shows on the powerful WSM reached every community in the South and beyond. *Opry* broadcasts were the Saturday night entertainment of black and white, rich and poor. When he dared dream of a national debut for Elvis, Sam saw the *Opry*. However, when the *Opry* thought new talent, it wasn't the raucousness of Elvis Presley. But Sam was persistent and while the band spent September playing the Eagle's Nest and any other place they could, the producer was fixing them a spot beyond their imaginations.

They piled in Sam's car to drive to Nashville on Saturday, October 2, Bill's beat up bass strapped on the roof. Elvis still played a child's guitar. The *Opry* gave them one song during the Hank Snow segment. It had been a hop, skip, and a jump from the Bon Air to the Overton Park Shell to the *Opry*, but their legs weren't very steady. When previously facing something bigger than themselves, they hit the ground running, and they did the same at the Ryman Auditorium. But the audience wasn't filled with teenagers, and Nashville hadn't been inundated with Sun #209 like Memphis had. Elvis, Scotty, and Bill quickly fell into their routine, but the audience wouldn't be pushed. Elvis felt like he did after his Bon Air debut: Because he hadn't torn off the roof, he had not succeeded.

Scotty Moore: 'We were all scared to death. Here we come with two little funky instruments and a whole park full of people, and Elvis, instead of just standing flat-footed and tapping his foot, well, he was kind of jiggling. That was just his way of tapping his foot. Plus I think with those old loose britches that we wore – they weren't pegged, they had lots of material and pleated fronts – you shook your leg, and it made it look like all hell was going on under there.'

In some tarpaper shack in a cotton field, in the drawing room of a gracious antebellum home, in the kitchen of several burger joints in several different cities, when the sound of Elvis, Scotty, and Bill came over the Hayride, heads turned and eyes met. Lives changed.

Milestone Dates: October 16th, 1954 — Louisiana Hayride

The nearest competition to the *Grand Ole Opry* was a broadcast out of Shreveport, Louisiana, the *Louisiana Hayride*. They were less stringent in their music classifications, a little more open-minded and willing to take a chance. They not only wanted Elvis on their show, they wanted him as a regular.

Elvis had released his second single, 'Good Rockin' Tonight,' the week before his *Opry* appearance, doubling his known repertoire. He was still nervous, still used 'That's All Right' to kick off his *Hayride* appearance, and was received only fair on the first show; the second show that night, he got the response he needed. Every bit as important as the applause was the demand the broadcast would create for his live show. Those performers who could not roll with Elvis and the changing tide had to begin concentrating on gigs beyond the Hayride's reach.

They became regulars on the weekly *Hayride*, driving the eight or so hours from Memphis in Scotty's Chevrolet. As leader, Elvis was paid eighteen dollars per appearance, with Bill and Scotty each receiving twelve. The bigger payoff was in steady-gigging. The Texas panhandle tumbles into the late November Houston Hoedown, where they were held over for two extra nights. Bob Neal, a Memphis disc jockey, began booking them, small towns and smaller ones. But lots of them, and Elvis and Scotty and Bill wanted to play.

A Solid Team
Nineteen fifty-five kicked off with a tour of West Texas under the auspices of the Louisiana Hayride, then on to the Mid-South with Bob Neal. Audiences didn't know how to react when they first encountered Elvis. He was well past his stage jitters, if not yet a master of crowd control. I am here, his first chord announced. You are there, the band kicked in. But let's all of us get real real gone, his stage show said. And people weren't used to being hit over the head. The moves Elvis had adopted from black culture were foreign to these eyes. When he landed on the stages of these small towns and even in the big cities, backwater redneck and slick city Jack and Jane were both blindsided by the gale force of the future. How were they supposed to know? How were they supposed to react? Bill was there to rescue the audiences that got too stunned, ready to hambone it up and tell a few jokes, give a reference point to people who saw static, heard white noise, and were breathing shallow through their mouths. Scotty kept it musical, sincere, interesting to the trained ear and melodic to the casual listener. They were a solid team.

Merle Kilgore, a fellow Louisiana Hayride musician: 'I think he scared them a little. He was really on the toes of his feet singing. I think they thought he was going to jump off the stage. But when he came back out, he destroyed them – by now they knew he wasn't going to jump off the stage and beat them, and they absolutely exploded.'

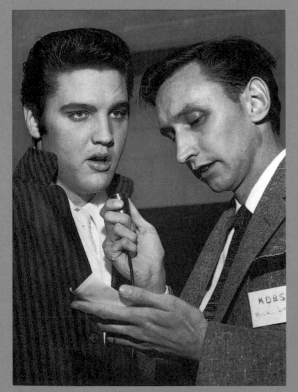

Elvis is interviewed off stage at the *Hayride*

The Hayride was serious competition for the Opry, broadcasting with a 50,000 watt clear-channel signal that could reach no less than twenty-eight states. On the third Saturday of each month, they tied in with CBS and were broadcast for an hour into 198 of the network's stations nationwide.

Scotty, DJ and Bill back Elvis on a *Hayride* session

1954-55 The Hillbilly Cat

On February 6, they had a homecoming of sorts, playing two shows at Ellis Auditorium, a Memphis venue Elvis had often attended as a dreamy-eyed kid. They were fourth on a bill, ranking above the Wilburn Brothers and Jim Ed and Maxine Brown, below 'Beautiful Gospel Singer' Martha Carson, Ferlin Husky and headliner Faron Young. Their third single had been out about a month and they were looking at steady dates ahead. Elvis had his first adult guitar.

Between shows at a meeting arranged by Bob Neal, who could feel the act going beyond his booking capabilities, Elvis was introduced to Colonel Tom Parker. Parker's history included managing Eddy Arnold and Hank Snow, and booking major country music tours through his Jamboree Attractions. Those who had been following Elvis knew he was going to go national because wherever he went, people reacted. Elvis Presley set fires within.

Their constant playing made it easier for new songs to creep into their set, and there was no lack of material. And what they were playing was made secondary by how they were playing it.

They toured in Scotty's car, each taking turns behind the wheel. Scotty drove like he played, steady and consistently. Bill's stories always made time fly faster, except those he told while driving, and then the others worried about having a wreck. Elvis drove the way he danced, lurching across the South at varying speeds, constantly fiddling with the radio. Wait a minute, this station don't move me. Sometimes Jimmie Rodgers Snow rode with them, or the lovely Anita Carter, who brought out the flirt in each. If it was a Bob Neal tour, he sometimes accompanied them, occasionally bringing his own car, and also sometimes his wife. And always plenty of promo pictures which he would hawk around to the crowd.

Neal went with them in late February to Cleveland, Ohio. They played the Circle Theater Jamboree, discovering that audiences in the North reacted much like those in the South and West. In mid-March, they flew to New York – the first time in a plane for Elvis and Bill – to audition for Arthur Godfrey, who was not interested. Back on the road, they sported a 1951 Cosmopolitan Lincoln, which Bill totalled within a few weeks.

Anticipation

Elvis was learning about anticipation. He wanted his audience to explode – indeed much of his audience came because his shows allowed them to explode – but he wanted to heat them slowly to the boiling point. He soon found that when he stepped onto the stage, the people were so eager for his act that half of it was just his presence. Instead of running out and kicking into the opening song, he initiated foreplay, standing still, so that just tapping his leg generated screams. Another single, another tour. Being on the road could be as exciting as it could be exhausting, sleeping in the back seat, sleeping backstage, rushing to the next city, next gig, next state, but if it's Saturday, it must be Shreveport. Unless otherwise noted.

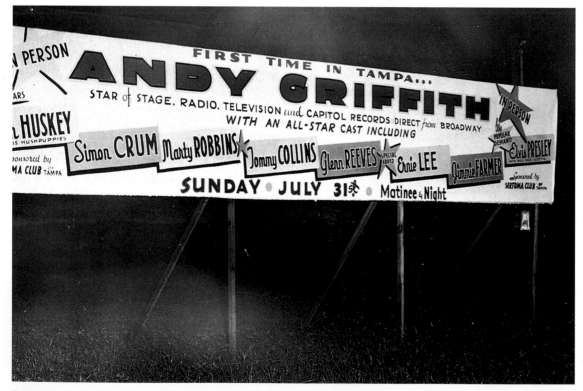

Celebrity Andy Griffith headlined one of Colonel Parker's package shows, Elvis is 'by popular demand'

Tampa Florida, and this time it's Andy Griffith, who would soon make his initial foray into feature films in A Face In The Crowd, portraying Lonesome Rhodes, a southern, backwoods singer whose meteoric rise into American culture is paved with manipulation and turpitude.

Elvis on stage – with some serious amplification – for his spot on the Andy Griffith tour show

In Jacksonville, Florida, all hell finally broke loose. Having mastered the slow boil, Elvis tested his control, inviting the girls in the audience of 14,000 to join him backstage. Like spies, they found the one unlocked window, and by the time the cops rescued him, Elvis had lost his boots and socks, his jacket and shirt were in tatters, his belt was gone, and they were starting on his pants. It was the beginning of a riot that would last until August 16, 1977.

At a Fourth of July picnic in Texas, Elvis was scheduled to perform twice on a bill that included an old favorite influence of his, the Blackwood Brothers. Hanging around with them backstage – idols he'd playfully dreamed of someday meeting – and overcome by the innocence and sincerity of the families lounging on blankets, the kids running around spitting watermelon seeds at each other, the pretty pink dresses and the bonnets to keep out the sun, he greeted the expectations for his misunderstood, lurid, Americana with a set of gospel songs, praise Jesus, a set of his boyhood favorites from the Assembly of God, amen. The reception from the audience was flat – gong – and for the second show, fueled by the oncoming power of the evening's darkness, he satisfied both those yearning to thrill at his manic energy and torrid movements, and those just itching to be offended by them.

Homecoming

A return to Texas and Florida, the Colonel's domain, Dallas and the 'Big D Jamboree,' yet another car and another headliner. From Tampa, Florida to Sheffield, Alabama, the Colonel to Bob Neal, a five-day tour that introduced Johnny Cash and also featured Webb Pierce and Wanda Jackson. Elvis was singing his way to a Memphis homecoming at the Overton Park Shell, once again appearing right before the headliner – Webb Pierce instead of Slim Whitman – only this time Elvis is tried, true, and triumphant. Sam Phillips was not foreign to crowd-boiling himself, releasing 'Mystery Train' to coincide with the event.

Country singer Bob Luman, about a show in the Spring of 1955: 'This cat came out in red pants and a green coat and a pink shirt and socks, and he had this sneer on his face and he stood behind the mike for five minutes, I'll bet, before he made a move. Then he hit his guitar a lick, and he broke two strings. Hell, I'd been playing ten years, and I hadn't broken a total of two strings. So there he was, these two strings dangling, and he hadn't done anything except break the strings yet, and these high school girls were screaming and fainting and running up to the stage, and then he started to move his hips real slow like he had a thing for his guitar...'

Parker booked them on a ten-day tour that began in Roswell, New Mexico. Hank Snow topped, with the Carter Sisters, Hank's son Jimmie Rodgers Snow, plus comedian the Duke of Paducah.

The auditorium awaits Elvis; the venue is the Fort Homer Hesterly Armory, Tampa

Elvis would love to stick around the hometown and hang with the homeboys, folks, but Elvis – has – left – the – ci-ty. Hightailing it from Memphis to Shreveport, the Hayride, where his appearances were now becoming less regular. Might as well hit Texas again while we're here. Now carrying a fourth member, drummer D. J. Fontana, and signed with the Colonel as a regular part of his Jamboree Attractions. The Colonel renegotiated the Hayride contract, changing, among other agreements, the fee, which went up nearly five times its previous amount.

September allowed a day off from performing once a week, but those were devoted to travelling, roadrunning from the Tennessee-Virginia border to Shreveport, beep beep. East coast, Texas desert, the lucky mid-West where for more than a week in October of 1955, fans of the musical style that had defied genres and now was becoming not just a sound but a movement could hear on a single bill for one night in each town and one night only the unbelievable pairing of the two foremost purveyors of rock'n'roll, Bill Haley and his Comets and Elvis Presley with the Blue Moon Boys.

Triumph

In mid-November, the band enjoyed another triumphant return home, once again playing a familiar environ – Ellis Auditorium – but this time as the headliner. Introduced on the bill was Sun Records newcomer Carl Perkins, who was soon to release 'Blue Suede Shoes.' Hank Thompson and Carl Smith also performed. The hometown crowd came out in full support, and the band rewarded them by lingering at the stage after the show, chatting and signing autographs.

Elvis didn't have time to stick around, but backstage negotiations between all advisors and management had been heated, tense, and action-packed. Eight days after Ellis he was back in Memphis, November 21, back at Sun, this time flailing an inkpen instead of a guitar, signing a contract to move from Sun to the roster of RCA Victor. The bounty on his head set a new record as the highest paid for any entertainer in recorded history. That same week at a disc jockey convention in Nashville, he was named 'Up and Coming Most Programmed Male Vocalist.' And while all that was great news, it didn't keep him from four more Hayride shows before year's end, appearances in Texas, Georgia, and Alabama, and, as a sign of his gratitude and respect, a Christmas pageant put on by an old teacher at Humes High.

Cashbox: 'Presley has been the rage of the country 'bobby-soxers' wherever he has performed. In addition, the chanter has been a double threat on wax inasmuch as his platters have a rhythm and blues flavoring and have been spilling over into that field and it's also quite possible that the versatile Presley could well become a big pop name.'

The Memphis Press-Scimitar ran a large article about Elvis in advance of the show, not yet granting him the front page but taking him from the entertainment section into the national news.

Andy Griffith himself takes the stage

The Pelvis

1956 The Pelvis

Nineteen fifty six was the year of dreams, the year of rags to riches, the myth of America personified. Elvis began the year anticipating a steady gig on the *Hayride* and the regular round of touring. But 1956 quickly became the year of television, then the year of Las Vegas, then Hollywood, and culminated as the year of the millionaire.

Nineteen fifty six was the year of television. Newly signed to RCA, the fireball from the *Louisiana Hayride* was booked on television's *Stage Show*. People remained unsure what to make of the band: Bill Black's yarn-spinning country warmth, Scotty's jazz-flavored guitar, D. J.'s beat-heavy drums, and the blues that ate the soul of Elvis Presley. But promoters knew which show was drawing the crowds. 'The Most Talked About New Personality In The Last Ten Years Of Recorded Music,' his ads boasted. And when required, he still did four shows a day.

The band flew to New York for their TV debut. There wasn't time to drive back and forth in Elvis' pink and black Cadillac sedan or his canary yellow Caddie convertible. On *Stage Show*, the group were again playing to an audience unfamiliar with their show and unsure how to react. Elvis shook a lot for a singer, and though he appeared to be having fun, his sneer caused confusion. He reeled back from the microphone, swinging his guitar, and the audience was silent. They applauded Scotty's guitar solo, and when Elvis next danced with his instrument he too was cheered. A milestone in an incredible success story, their TV debut is, in retrospect, heart-wrenchingly innocent. They're four guys showing America what they learned from the crossroads of culture that is Memphis, Tennessee. From this peak, they can't help looking back, knowing how far they've come, but we can't help looking forward, knowing where they'll go.

Days after his premiere, in Norfolk, Virginia, he was billed above Hank Snow and grossed twelve thousand dollars for his night's work. Almost ten thousand people saw him over the course of three shows that day, and his records were suddenly selling 100,000 copies per week. *Stage Show* booked him for six dates within eight weeks.

The Colonel kept Elvis on the road, now with a *Grand Ole Opry* tour, then on his own, out aga in with Hank Snow. One show today, four shows tomorrow, back to New York. East Coast, top to bottom. In Charlotte, North Carolina, fans shredded all his clothes except his pants, and they'd managed to loosen the cuffs from those. They'd taken the tassels from his shoes, his watch, his ring. A headline in Jacksonville, Florida: 'Elvis Presley Collapses.' He still wanted to greet

---

Carolina Theater review, 2/17/56: 'Mr. Presley must be seen to be believed – and even then he seems somewhat unbelievable. He plays ("beats" would be a better word) the guitar. He sings (almost any other word would be better there) He slouches; he scratches; he mugs; he bumps and grinds. He brings to the stage one of the most monumental conceits seen in these parts in many a day.'

Presley Drives 'Em Wi-uld

His Singin' And Wigglin' Sends Fans

By NORTON MOCKRIDGE, Staff Writer.

The Elvis Presley style of guitar playing.

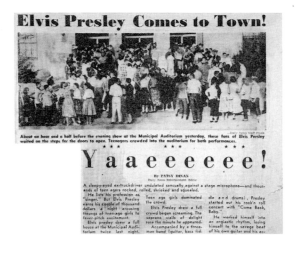

Elvis Presley Comes to Town!

About an hour and a half before the evening show at the Municipal Auditorium yesterday, these fans of Elvis Presley waited on the steps for the doors to open. Teenagers crowded into the auditorium for both performances.

★ ★ ★   ★ ★ ★   ★ ★ ★

Yaaeeeeee!

By PATSY DINAN

Stage Show was a half-hour variety tv programme hosted by bandleaders the Dorsey Brothers. Perry Como's more established show competed in the same slot, so Elvis was booked for January 28th 1956.

The CBS Studios displaying the *Stage Show* line-up of the Dorseys, Sarah Vaughan... and Elvis

1956 The Pelvis

Elvis Presley: 'Sure they tear off my clothes, they scratch their initials on my cars, they phone my hotel all night. But they buy my records and they pay to see me sing. I'm grateful and when they stop annoying me, I'll start to worry... I've got money for a haircut, but this is good business. It's important that I be conspicuous... I don't think it's right for a fellow to dress loud. On the street that is. On the stage, I want to stand out. The louder my clothes, the better.'

Earl Wilson, a syndicated New York columnist: 'He's got a voice that's very loud and full of feeling and when he sings, unlike Como, it is not effortless. Like Johnny Ray, to whom he has been compared, he writhes and contorts and suffers through a song, and the kids love it... He wears his hair long, with sideburns yet.'

Elvis in action during his second appearance on the *Milton Berle Show*

his fans, to honor his debt to those who'd helped make his rise so meteoric. He wanted to, but he fell out from exhaustion, hospitalized overnight but insistent on fulfilling his February 25th obligation.

A month later, still touring, now with a complete album of his music available, the band pulled into Lexington, Kentucky. Checking into a hotel, they slept for the day. Elvis awoke with a fever a doctor diagnosed influenza. Elvis performed as scheduled, ushered by policemen through a crowd, onto the stage, where his ferocity was apparently undiminished, where the wiggling evoked screams, where pauses were filled by female shouts of longing, and the boys in the audience just studied the moves.

The appearances with the Dorsey Brothers had brought Elvis into thousands of households, but that program did not compare to the power wielded by Milton Berle. Elvis may have dressed conservatively, but the bold tie and the sideburns were dead giveaways. They performed a sultry version of the just-released 'Heartbreak Hotel,'

and Elvis' left leg quickly became the center of attention. When it was time for Scotty's guitar solo, Elvis reeled back, shaking his instrument and doing a little jig. But the screams really erupted when he swung his guitar aside, held out his left hand and, just like the fan dancers working under the red lights, he strutted his hunk o' stuff.

Frenzy

His appearance with Milton Berle was followed by two sold out shows in San Diego, performing for five thousand happy fans and hundreds more who were turned away at the door, his eight song set raking in $15,000 in ticket revenues.

A special squad from the shore patrol was called in to protect Elvis, and they created a flying wedge formation to get him out of the arena. Elvis' entourage, in fact, did include an Elvis lookalike who, after the shows, was fed to the lions, diverting the crowd's attention so the real singer could escape. Fans could no longer distinguish between pain and pleasure, evident

Denver 4/10/56: 'A performance by Elvis Presley goes something like this: Elvis strides on stage, takes a wide legged stance, grabs up a guitar, gives it a couple of whangs, opens his mouth and starts gyrating. Elvis' stage maneuvers are nothing short of phenomenal. He shivers and shakes, he quivers and quakes. The faster Elvis Presley moves, the more agitated the crowd grows. When he sings a slower tune with some melody and practically no shaking, the crowd doesn't react. When he starts to shake, the crowd bursts into a frenzy of squeals... during Sunday night's intermission a crow laden with glossy photos of Presley paraded the aisles selling the pictures to eager customers. Sales for Presley pictures were almost as brisk as the popcorn concession.'

On April 3rd 1956, Uncle Milty, 'The Father of Television,' broadcast his show from the USS Hancock in San Diego harbour, and Elvis Presley was thrust directly into the mainstream of American popular culture.

Another treat for our boys!
TONIGHT— Direct from the flight deck of the aircraft carrier U.S.S. Hancock in San Diego Harbor...
THE MILTON BERLE SHOW
starring
MILTON BERLE • ESTHER WILLIAMS
HARRY JAMES and his orchestra
with BUDDY RICH at the drums
ELVIS PRESLEY America's newest singing sensation
ARNOLD STANG • VICTOR YOUNG and his orchestra
Same time as usual-
TONIGHT— 8 to 9
Channel 4

1956 The Pelvis

in the blossoming young ladies who used dull knives to carve Elvis' name into their arms. When Colonel Tom took over the photo concession from Bill Black, it was just as well – Bill was going to get hurt just getting so close to the fans.

During the midwestern tour that followed California, society witnessed a frenzy new to its collective consciousness. It reached such extremes that Elvis was forced to distance himself from his fans, from those to whom he wanted to remain closest, for their own safety as much as for his. In Wichita, Kansas, the headline after his April 13th show read, 'Singer Big Hit – Only One Injured.' The story was of a girl waiting at the front of a teeming, stage door throng who had her arm shoved through a glass window. 'I guess it was worth it,' she said. Another wire report around that time told of a young femme who lay atop her bunk bed and listened dreamily to Elvis records; a photograph of her in the hospital ran in many newspapers, her collarbone broken when she slipped, while leaning down to flip the record.

Crescendo

The night after Wichita, in Amarillo, Texas, the excitement hit a crescendo even before he took the stage. Just waiting for the Municipal Auditorium to open, fans worked themselves to a riotous state, smashing a locked door. When he finally performed, the screaming began before he could reach his microphone. The natural restraint of 'Baby Let's Play House' made a good opener, leaving him a place to carry them. The blue and red floodlights enhanced the moodiness of 'Heartbreak Hotel,' the guitar breaks being an indication of what was to come: 'Long Tall Sally' and 'I Got A Woman,' before catching his breath with 'I Was the One' and 'Only You,' and then finally allowing the release of madness, time to step over the line, to push the person in front of you, to be pushed from behind, to cross the bounds of politeness, to move like the man on stage, to remove any social constraints completely from your consciousness, to rock, and to roll: 'Blue Suede Shoes.'

When done, those too exhausted or with parents too strict filed out to fall out at home. But those who had had so much that they had to have more, junkies for Elvis – he sent them to a place in themselves that they never knew existed, and they wanted – HAD TO HAVE – m-m-m-more, they congregated at the stage door, feeding off each other's adrenaline, relishing the smashing of glass panes, some relieving themselves of the beast within by trampling the hoods of a couple Cadillacs parked nearby, thinking they might belong to Elvis (they did not), anything so their lives might have an impact on his like his was having on theirs. 'We want Elvis!' they demanded as one, persistent, feeling themselves slipping from that place within, needing his presence to remain there. Needing his presence. And he did finally appear, nonchalantly donned in a mandarin-collared gray print silk shirt, cerise swing-back jacket, black trousers and black moccasins. The huge humping throng of fans forced Elvis to flee. An incident two days later in San Antonio forced

Was he stung by a hornet or singed by a "hot-foot"? ... No, he's just one of the agitated Elvis Presley fans.

Gal 'Takes It Off' as Elvis Presley Does 'Cooch'

Elvis began to get top billing over the Louvin Brothers (who were his mother's favourite group), the Carter Sisters, and Justin Tubb – all established names.

The Elvis Presley Show comes to town, complete with fake cactus and bales of hay

Elvis to give up meeting his fans. The *San Antonio Light* headline was 'Atomic Powered Presley Bombs S. A,' and the article stated, 'Behind him he left tears, screams, wild applause, mangled emotions – in short, agony, sweet and complete. It was a traumatic experience this newly arrived singing star brought.' Wearing a white silk jacket, black trousers, and a blue satin shirt with a mandarin collar, he added to his set 'Money Honey' and 'Tutti Frutti.' At the show's completion, his team set up a table in front of the backstage door and asked the uncontrollable mob to line up for autographs, please. That proved a harsh return to reality, the table becoming just an object to be smashed up against.

After Elvis left Corpus Christi, despite the lack of damage to the Memorial Coliseum and Exposition Hall, the city barred further rock and roll shows there. In Oklahoma City, the chairman of the Board of Censors attended the afternoon show and, realizing he could have a riot on his hands, allowed the evening show as scheduled.

Vegas

Nineteen fifty six became the year of Las Vegas. Six months after storming the *Grand Ole Opry,* he conquered another entertainment landmark, booked for a two week engagement at the Frontier Hotel's appropriately sci-fi designed Venus Room. His detractors recall that after his first night as headliner, he was made opening act for comedian Shecky Green and the smooth strains of Freddie Martin's big band.

They do not mention that he still sold out every show, nor that he quickly appreciated that the Vegas audience was completely unlike his usual audience: These people, for God's sake, intended to *dine* while he performed!

Two weeks in one place gave Elvis and the band a chance to relax, travel time replaced with free time. They had become accustomed to the night hours, which suited Vegas. Elvis slept late, eating breakfast at 4:30 PM. (Half a cantaloupe with ice cream, then a full spread with extra bacon on the side, then another half a cantaloupe with

The Frontier (left) and Johnny Cash backstage

ice cream.) When he went out, sharing the town with the world's entertainment elite, he remained a center of attention. A Vegas columnist trailed him for a day, and noted that when Elvis tried on clothes in a men's shop, he did it in front of hundreds of curiosity seekers pressed against the window. A different crowd gaped as he entertained himself on the bumper cars at the Last Frontier Village – for five hours. In the privacy of his own room, Elvis was surrounded by an entourage, and when he entered the Venus Room for his show, everything stopped – eating, chewing, the clattering of silverwear. The journalist was amazed that a person could endure such loss of privacy.

In Port Arthur, Canada, a disc jockey purposely played an Elvis record at the wrong speed, and was greeted in the station's lobby by seven leather-jacketed hoodlums who warned him he should not leave work that night.

Several months earlier, Elvis would not have been old enough to enter the room that was now paying him $12,500 per week. Winning over these sophisticates who would take pride in spurning his plebeian popularity meant a throwback to his long ago days of playing crowds unfamiliar and unprepared for him, crowds too shocked to know how to respond. Opening with 'Blue Suede Shoes' brought scattered applause, but as he proceeded, as they become accustomed to the new stage language, the audience became more enthusiastic. During his stint, there was a special Saturday show for teens at the Venus Room.

Rumors

Another indication of his popularity were the rumors which seemed as numerous as his records: he was going to die, he was pushing dope, he wore lady's underwear, he had served time – all of which he was forced to deny and laugh off. Less often noted were the actual perils, such as the time his chartered plane gassed up in Fort Smith, Arkansas and the attendant did not attend the center tank, so that when the pilot switched to it in mid-flight, the plane hung there a moment and they all faced death. And if the tens of thousands of miles he covered were reported, one still could not grasp how the wear and tear affected him, the loss of sleep, the resulting nervousness, a weight-gain of thirty pounds in one year. It may have been his lack of concentration or it may have been the sudden affluence after years of poverty, but a member of Elvis' entourage was assigned to check every room Elvis departed, looking in hotel drawers and backstage dressing rooms for wads of cash that he may have set down and forgotten.

On May 15th, Elvis returned to Memphis to play Ellis Auditorium during the Cotton Carnival. Finally he was receiving front page attention, royal treatment, arriving at the show in a limousine with a police escort. His fans hooted during the acts that preceded him, punctuating the intermissions with chants of 'We want Elvis.' In Memphis, when he announced he would be returning to the city for a benefit show on the Fourth of July, the auditorium nearly went into orbit.

'Presley, who adds an extra thrust to his vocals is the ultimate in the exploitation of what is essentially trashy material.'

Elvis with his group and (top) the Jordanaires

Security tightens as the concerts get more hectic

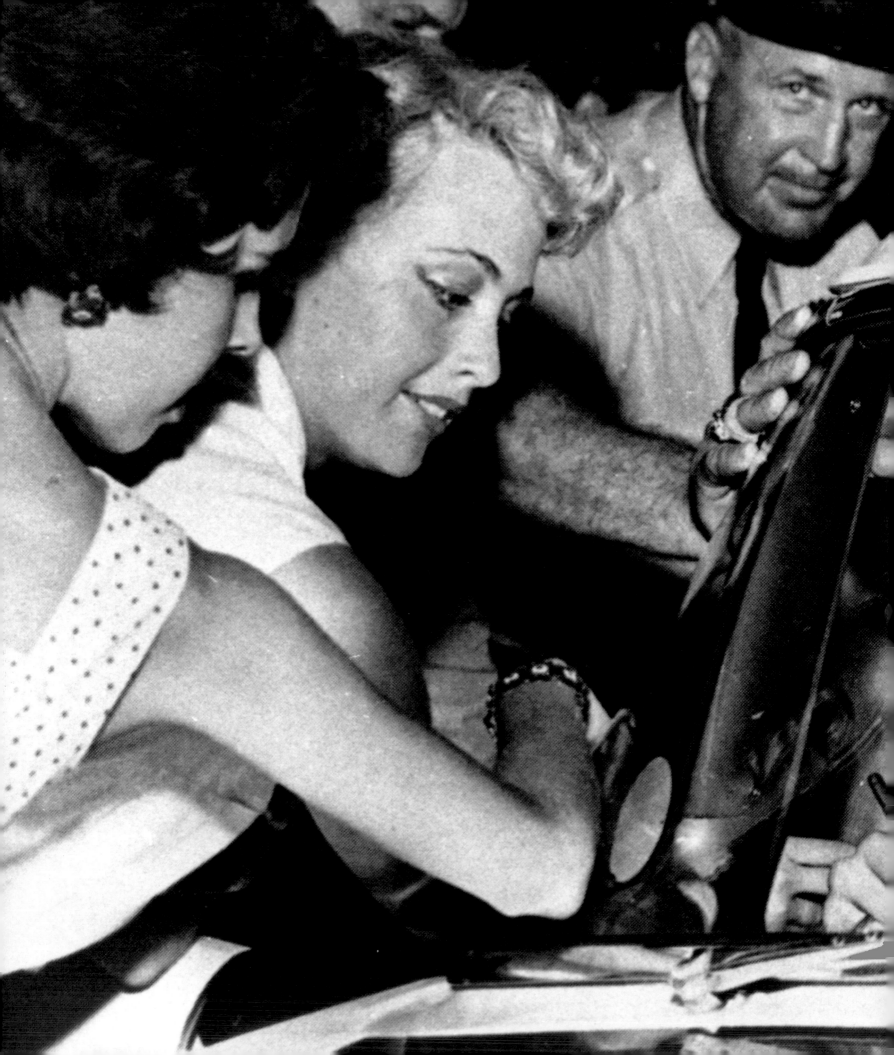

1956 The Pelvis

Sharing

The summer kicked off with another appearance on Milton Berle, which garnered a whole new legion of fans. As the featured act, Elvis was drawing steadily increasing audiences: 7,000, 8,000, 10,000. Ed Sullivan steadfastly refused to pander to such immoral impulses, but Steve Allen presented him in a tux. Elvis' deferential treatment to Allen outshone the host's attempt to break the young buck. After the broadcast, Elvis phoned in an interview to the show *Hy Gardner Calling*, using the opportunity to dispel the recurring rumors of drugs and sexual perversion.

The band completed another recording session while they were in New York, then Elvis took a train to Memphis, where the anticipation for his July 4th gig was steady-building steam. Seven thousand people packed the baseball park, many of them arriving early in the morning, meals packed, to get good seats. The three hours of entertainment that preceded Elvis included appearances by Eddie Rocker, Wink Martindale,

and La Gitana Nancy Long, who did unsupported splits on a pedestal. The show was hosted by Dewey Phillips, whose antics included what may be the first publicly staged Elvis impersonations, ribbing him about the monkey suit he'd worn for Steve Allen. When Dewey finally brought Elvis out to the audience that had only recently recovered from his appearance seven weeks before, they established a new capacity for frenzy. A few people heard the proclamation making it Elvis Presley Day, and he confided – and *there* is the secret, that despite the mayhem created by all those individuals crowded together, he could make each one believe he was sharing something with him or her only – he confided that New York (meaning everyone everywhere outside of those who *knew*), that he wasn't going to let New York change him. His thirty minutes ended with the chaos-inducing 'Hound Dog,' and then he dove into a police car waiting beside the stage, the escape proving that, despite the smarmy Steve Allen, things were indeed like they'd always been.

Robert Johnson, Memphis Press-Scimitar 7/5/56: 'Police Capt. Fred Woodward brought Elvis to Russwood in a white squad car about mid-way during the first act of the show, but fans out front heard Elvis was there, began flanking around the squad car and besieged it. Capt. Woodward had to drive him out of the park again and return just before Elvis went on stage. When Elvis finally went on stage, pandemonium broke out. His fans broke from their seats, swept like a wave up to the stage, despite efforts of police, firemen and Shore Patrolmen. Elvis pleaded with them as pleasantly as he could to sit down, but it was like Canute telling the tide to stop...'

Everywhere Elvis played, the fans got more frantic, the events more chaotic

'The carnage was terrific. After the show, bedlam! He fled to the insufficient sanctuary of his suite. The door wouldn't hold them out. They got his shirt, and it was shredded. A girl seized a button, clutched it as though it were a diamond.'

1956 The Pelvis

Elvis got to relax a bit after that, not appearing on a stage again until the 3rd of August, when he began a Florida tour that would end just before he was due in Hollywood, shooting on his first film starting August 22nd. Nineteen fifty six became the year of Hollywood. While in Vegas, Elvis had seen the last of his boyhood dreams burst into reality: Hollywood calling Mr. Presley, Hollywood offering a role in *The Rainmaker*, Hollywood putting Elvis Presley beside Burt Lancaster and Katherine Hepburn. Mr. Presley and his manager's response: Thank you. But no thank you. The role is not right. And thus *Love Me Tender*.

Midway through shooting, Elvis appeared on *The Ed Sullivan Show*. Appropriately, he gave a sneak preview of 'Love Me Tender,' stunning his audience with the smooth ballad. Returning for 'Ready Teddy,' he rocked out. A petition was circulated calling Elvis 'vulgar, suggestive, and disgusting,' asking the courts to ban him from TV. The public responded with a record-breaking one million advance orders of the new ballad.

Jack Gould, New York Times 9/10/56 [reviewing the first appearance of Elvis on the Ed Sullivan television show]: 'Mr. Presley initially disturbed adult viewers – and instantly became a martyr in the eyes of his teenage following – for his strip tease behavior on last spring's Milton Berle program. Then with Steve Allen he was much more sedate. On the Sullivan program he injected movements of the tongue and indulged in wordless singing that were singularly distasteful… When Presley executes his bumps and grinds, it must be remembered by the Columbia Broadcasting System that even the 12-year-old's curiosity may be over-stimulated… The issue is not one of censorship, which solves nothing; it is one of common sense. It is no impingement on the medium's artistic freedom to ask the broadcaster merely to exercise good sense and display responsibility. It is no blue-nosed suppression of the proper way of depicting life in the theater to expect stage manners somewhat above the level of the carnival sideshow.'

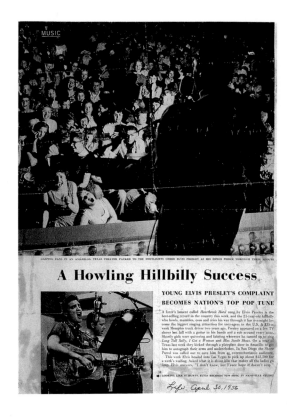

A Howling Hillbilly Success

YOUNG ELVIS PRESLEY'S COMPLAINT BECOMES NATION'S TOP POP TUNE

Crowds gather in anticipation of Elvis' appearance at the Florida Theatre, Jacksonville

Elvis posing with fans

One girl recounted: 'I grabbed his hand. He grinned and said, 'Cut me loose,' so I cut him loose. It was heavenly.'

Before finishing the film, Elvis played a triumphant homecoming in Tupelo at the Mississippi-Alabama Fair and Dairy Show, his first appearance there since he'd sung 'Ol'Shep' a lifetime ago. 'The fair this year has the strongest grandstand lineup in years,' boasted the *Tupelo Daily Journal*. 'It has Elvis Presley, the current biggest drawing card on the American entertainment scene; and it has an outstanding lineup of livestock and agricultural exhibits.' A wire report covering Elvis's September 26th show ran the headline: 'Tupelo Ain't Nothin' But a Town Agog.' The Governor and Mayor praised him from the stage, and Elvis said of his return, 'It's the greatest thing that's ever happened to me.' A fan rushed the stage while Elvis was singing 'I Got A Woman.' He fell backwards and laughed, and two police officers grabbed the sixteen year old and carried her kicking from the stage. When she was later asked why she'd stormed him, she replied, 'I want him and I need him and I love him.'

When the puppet master waved, the screams dutifully rose to shrieks.

In blue velvet shirt, black pants and blue suede shoes, he sent two 15,000 crowds into hysterics

TONIGHT ONLY
TUPELO'S OWN
ELVIS PRESLEY
8:00 P. M.
FAIRGROUNDS

MISS. ALA. FAIR & DAIRY SHOW
WELCOMES
TUPELO'S OWN - IN PERSON
ELVIS PRESLEY
WITH HIS OWN SHOW
FAIRGROUNDS
8:00 P. M.
FRIDAY SEP 27
ALL SEATS $2.00
BENEFIT ELVIS PRESLEY'S
YOUTH RECREATION CENTER
TO BE BUILT IN TUPELO
GET YOUR TICKETS EARLY
DON'T MISS IT

WELCOME
TUPELO'S OWN ELVIS

Back to Memphis, back to California, back on the road, this time by train, heading for a Texas tour which began October 11th at the Cotton Bowl in Dallas. A pre-show press interview was overrun by fan club presidents and their awestruck friends. During the half-hour, actual questions were sandwiched between squeals of, 'Oh! Elvis looked at me!' and 'Please just one more autograph, Elvis.'

Twenty six thousand five hundred fans packed the stadium. They endured Sherry David, Howard and Wanda Bell, Rex Marlowe, Hubert Castle, and finally the Jordanaires – all backed by Hyman Charinsky and his orchestra – before the spotlight hit the locker room area and found Elvis sitting atop the back of a Cadillac convertible moving toward the pink and black stage at the fifty-yard line. Clearly enjoying himself after his brief respite, he assumed his position at the microphone and waited for the pandemonium to settle into mere chaos. When it did, he threw his head back and laughed; the crowd went ballistic.

A young photographer with a sharp eye, Alfred Wertheimer, began shooting Elvis a few days before the Steve Allen show, and recognizing a beautiful subject, and a willing one, he stayed on for several weeks thereafter, shooting plentifully.

1956 The Pelvis

With the audience completely in his control, he set the pace for his thirty-five minute show with 'Long Tall Sally.' Fully spasmodic, the binding by Steve Allen was worlds away. When he slowed things with 'Love Me Tender,' the audience maintained their passion, shifting from rhythmic pounding to howls of ecstasy. Eighty cops tried to contain the crowd when Elvis leapt from the stage to the ground during 'Hound Dog,' falling on his knees, huge microphone clutched tightly to his lips, only as obscene as the climax to a tent revival. With the audience lost in hysteria, Elvis leapt into a waiting Caddie which roared out to the accompaniment of a wailing police motorcycle escort. The stadium lights were quickly turned up.

The box office take in Dallas was estimated at thirty thousand dollars, of which Elvis' organization was likely to get eighteen. In addition, the merchandising movement was in full swing, the assortment of essential items available to every fan included: photos, T-shirts, wallets, blue jeans, charm bracelets, costume jewelry, skimmer-pump-shoes, statuettes, skirts and jumpers, scarves, handkerchiefs, hats, belts, bolo ties, twenty-five cent biographies, sneakers, statuette bookends, various other shirts, record-affixed magazines, wristwatches, zipper jackets, sleepwear, and lipstick in Hound Dog orange and Tender pink.

In Waco, an electrical short-circuit produced an amplification problem and Elvis stopped his show, saying to the facility employees in the wings, 'Hey, uh, sir, could we get that whatchamacallit fixed. These people were nice enough to come on down tonight and we want to give 'em the best.'

Chewing gum, he performed two shows in Houston to 8000 fans each time. 'I believe in God. I advise young singers to have faith like I did,' he told a journalist. The next night in San Antonio, fans fell before him, some beating their heads on the floor. After he'd peeled out in a waiting green Ford which left rubber marks, several of the fans mounted the stage, just wallowing in the sweat where he'd stood.

A syndicated column quotes an unnamed psychiatrist: 'Elvis Presley's great appeal for teenagers is that the guy is supposedly an adult. But he doesn't behave like one. With his duck bill haircut, his twitches, his tics and his sloppy dress, he has cut himself off from the adult world.'

San Antonio News: 'One innocent looking miss who probably went to Sunday School that morning flew into a rage when police wouldn't let her talk to Presley in his dressing room. She had climbed down a cement wall to get at a window of the room. Then she opened the window, spotted Elvis and let out a piercing yell. A county officer pushed her back and shut the window. Whambo! She kicked out a reinforced pane.'

The Fox Theater, Detroit Michigan, where Elvis appeared May 25th 1956

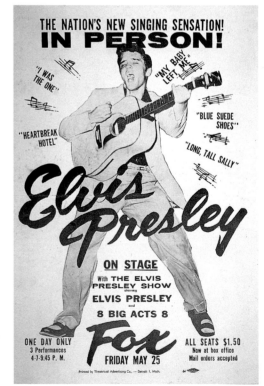

'He has a sulky look and his infrequent smile is almost surly...'

'No one'll replace him, even when we're married'

'His performance was the most disgusting exhibition this reporter has ever seen... He is the male counterpart of a hoochie-coochie dancer in a burlesque show'

THE POWER OF PRESLEY OVER HIS HOUSTON FOLLOWERS
Anguished, Adoring Expressions Were Typical at Coliseum Show
—Post Photo by Keith Newton

Houston Teen Agers Rocked By Presley

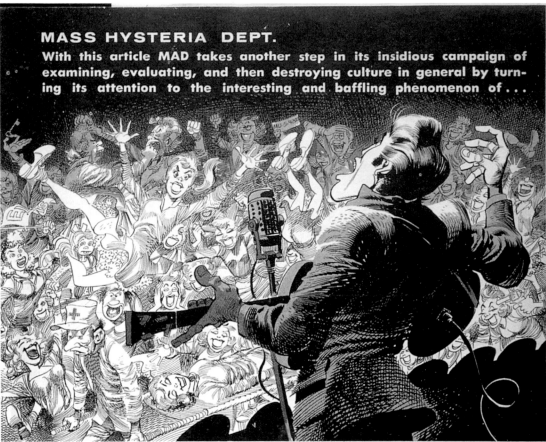

MASS HYSTERIA DEPT.
With this article MAD takes another step in its insidious campaign of examining, evaluating, and then destroying culture in general by turning its attention to the interesting and baffling phenomenon of...

'56

Gasping, shouting, and shrieking, audience of teen-agers leap from seats, dance in aisles, and stampede toward stage moment Elvis Pelvis strums electric guitar and begins to sing. Shrieking, dancing and stampeding reaction is due to teen-agers' sudden shocked discovery that electricity wired into Elvis's guitar is also wired into the audience seats.

FACIAL EXPRESSIONS DISPLAY GAMUT OF EMOTIONS

SAD LAMENT | PLAINTIVE SOB | WORRIED MOAN

PELVIS EXPOUNDS SAD LAMENT of the latest hit, "Standing By The Coroner."

PELVIS WAILS PLAINTIVE SOB of popular "On the Street Where You Lie."

PELVIS CHOKES WORRIED MOAN of the torch song, "I Almost Found My Mind."

2

ADVANCE SALE TICKET
COTTON BOWL STADIUM
OCT. Thurs., Oct. 11, 1956
RAIN OR SHINE
11 AT 8:00 P.M.
ELVIS PRESLEY
1956 SHOW
ADMISSION 1.14 $1.25
FEDERAL TAX .11
002301

ELVIS PRESLEY SHOW
October 11, 1956
AT 8:00 P.M.
"RAIN OR SHINE"
Cotton Bowl Stadium
RETAIN THIS STUB
Southwest Globe Ticket Co.—Dallas
002301

ELVIS PELVIS

In the music business, it seems that Perry Como, with his relaxed and flaccid style of singing, makes new friends and wins new plaudits each time he makes an appearance. On the other hand, it seems that Elvis Pelvis, with his frenzied shake, wriggle, squirm, rock and roll style of howling, makes new enemies and incites new objections each time he makes an appearance.

Since this kind of reaction is familiar to us (the same thing seems to happen in the magazine business each time MAD makes an appearance), your Editors attended a performance of said teen-age idol in order to see what gives. What gives, we observed, is Elvis's pelvis.

Candid pictures of Elvis, one-time hillbilly singer, show sensuous motions which punctuate sensuous lament. Sensuous motions and lament are caused by sentimental holdover from hillbilly days. Elvis still wears itchy flannel longjohns.

AS ELVIS PELVIS SINGS VARIOUS TYPES OF POP TUNES

| CAREFREE CHUCKLE | HAPPY GIGGLE | HYSTERICAL HOWL |

PELVIS LILTS CAREFREE CHUCKLE of the catchy "It Only Hurts When I Laugh!"

PELVIS CROONS HAPPY GIGGLE of the amusing ballad, "Electrocution Day."

PELVIS BELLOWS HYSTERICAL HOWL of revived "My Old Kentucky Home Brew."

* * There will probably never be another Yankee center fielder named Joe DiMaggio.

3

SANDRA FRIERY HAD STAR IN HER EYE
Elvis Puckered 50 Times
—Post Photo by Keith Hawkins

PRESLEY PERFORMS

Elvis received the ultimate compliment when the celebrated contortions of his stage act were satirised in Mad magazine.

On October 20th, 'Love Me Tender' was released as a single and entered the charts at number two, the highest-ever initial entry. It simultaneously entered the R&B charts at number eight and the country charts at number nine. On October 28th, a forty-foot cut-out of Elvis was unveiled atop the Paramount Theater in Times Square, publicizing the film's imminent release. Elvis himself was in attendance, before returning to Ed Sullivan's studio a few blocks away to continue rehearsing for his appearance that very night. The appearance was watched by 82.6% of the possible viewing audience, as compared to 78.6% who watched Dwight Eisenhower accept his presidential renomination.

On the eve of his film debut, Elvis attended a show by Liberace in Las Vegas. The two, whose common bond was pay scales and raiments, met backstage, where they exchanged sports jackets and instruments. 'Liberace can't compare with him,' one fan said. 'He doesn't move. If Elvis couldn't shake, he wouldn't be too good.'

Love Me Tender opened on November 15th in over 500 theaters. When Elvis appeared on the screen, fans in movie theaters reacted the same as they did at his shows.

Millions

Nineteen fifty six culminated as the year of the millionaire. Of RCA's twenty best sellers, fourteen were by Elvis. A Victor Records spokesperson said, 'We've got Decca and MGM pressing records for us right now because we can't handle it all.' *Variety* headline: 'Elvis A Millionaire in 1 Year.' The magazine attributed $100,000 to his TV stints, and $200,000 to his live shows. Record royalties were estimated at $450,000, and his movie deals at $250,000. The merchandising gross on fifty-one marketing licenses was estimated at $40,000,000 over fifteen months. Colonel estimated at the year's end that Elvis was responsible for a gross of twenty million during 1966. His personal income was estimated to be as high as $3,000,000.

One of Elvis' three appearances on the *Ed Sullivan*

'Everything happened so blame fast I don't know where I was yesterday and I don't know where I'll be tomorrow.'

A woman who'd ripped a button from Elvis' shirt put a classified ad in a newspaper, offering to sell it. She got more than 100 phone calls, and offers as high as $600. She decided to keep the button herself and took the phone off the hook.

In Memphis, Elvis took a girlfriend to see a late movie. When a group of teen girls spotted him, he had to dash into the theater, leaving his date to pick up the change. The girls mobbed his car, first as monkeys on a jungle gym, then as cats on a scratching post, and finally as schoolgirls. There was damage to the hood and fenders, the fine upholstery was shredded, and love messages written in lipstick covered the white exterior. The theater was showing newsreels of Elvis being mobbed by fans in Tupelo.

Thanksgiving, driving to Cleveland, the swanky Shalimar Room of the Commodore Perry Hotel and a bite to eat. One onlooker thought Elvis needed a knuckle sandwich, and he approached his table, saying, 'You [so-and-so], my wife carries a picture of you in her wallet, but she doesn't carry one of

Elvis made an appearance in a mezzanine window above the stage door. An ardent fan scaled the wall by holding the drain pipe, and he got an autograph. But the danger was obvious, and Elvis was quoted as saying, 'I get scared only when the audience starts hurting each other. That's why I stopped giving autographs.'

IN PERSON
ELVIS
PRESLEY
and His
ALL-STAR SHOW

SICK'S SEATTLE STADIUM
SUN., SEPT. 1st — 8:30 P. M.
$1⁵⁰ — $2⁵⁰ — $3⁵⁰

TICKETS AT —
SHERMAN CLAY

me. Let's step outside.' Before any steps were taken, the nineteen year-old Louis Balint let one fly, and fisticuffs ensued. When the cops arrived, Balint was reportedly trying to push Scotty Moore over the four-foot terrace railing. Two days later, Balint admitted from jail he'd been set up by a prankster. His wife, in fact, did not carry a picture of Elvis nor did she much care for his singing.

Peace in the valley
But by then, that uproar was long past for Elvis, whose ears were attuned to the throbbing crowd of 8,500 at each of his November 25th Louisville shows. Not included in that number were the 100 cops or the sixty ushers. 'I never knew I had so many fans in the Louisville Police Department,' Elvis quipped from the stage. The cops found that funnier than his stage movements, which they'd restricted to forth and back only – none of that sideways stuff, Mr. Presley. Elvis' father's parents were in the Louisville audience, and for them, their lewd grandson sang 'Peace In The Valley.'

Joking with the new audience, he said, 'You bring a lump – to my billfold.' Driving home from Louisville, Elvis grew tired and stopped at Colonel Parker's home in Madison, Tennessee, where he slept on the sofa. The next day, when his car's water pump went out between Nashville and Memphis, he slipped unnoticed into a roadside hotel and got another good night's sleep.

His last big gig of the year was a triumphant return to the Louisiana Hayride, performing a benefit there on December 15th for the Shreveport YMCA and its metropolitan expansion program. The event was held at the fairgrounds Youth Center to an overflowing audience of 9000. Once again, his press conference was overrun by fans, and little information was exchanged. He wore white shoes with blue soles, a green coat, blue pants and white shirt, a tie and a silk scarf – and he slayed them. Uncle Sam had notified him he was choice meat, but Elvis still had a few shows before someone else was to determine what color outfit he wore.

A 14 year old female fan reported to Louisville journalist: 'I knew weeks and weeks in advance that today would be the greatest day of my life. I planned and planned for it and I was one of the first to get tickets. Two weeks ago, I started trying to get hold of handcuffs. I thought I'd go up to Elvis after the show for his autograph. when he reached out, I'd snap the cuffs and we'd be sealed together… But nobody in town would sell me handcuffs.'

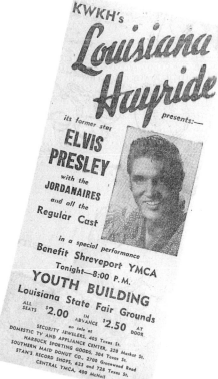

One fan, caught sneaking backstage, collapsed in sobs and begged, 'Oh, God. Just let me touch him. I can't stand it. Please, oh please just let me touch him. I've just got to touch him…'

The King of Rock'n'Roll

Elvis rocked into the new year with his third performance on the *Ed Sullivan Show*. Appearances on national television were becoming as common to him as the local stage used to be.

His January 6th Sullivan engagement came amid rumors of his waning popularity. Elvis had succeeded despite lashings from the print media, and they did not miss this opportunity to fuel the roiling feud. Though the network censored Elvis, shooting him only from above the hips, the show's host used the occasion to clear himself of past transgressions. After Elvis performed 'Peace In the Valley,' Sullivan interrupted his show's smooth flow to announce to viewers everywhere: '...this is a real decent, fine boy...' 'Decent,' Sullivan said, and millions of Americans heard him clearly.

By late March, four months had passed since Elvis' last tour. Fans may have been experiencing withdrawal symptoms, but the factory was working overtime, edgy about the looming military call. Elvis had submerged himself in Hollywood to make

'He'd laugh... partly at himself...

... and partly at the audience'

'He seemed to deliberately push the button by dropping his arm or wiggling his shoulder, just to hear his fans react'

The New York World Telegram commented: 'If his performance is evil, then so is the classic ballet in which raw sex – tightly attired – is the backbone.'

1957-61 The King of Rock'n'Roll

Loving You. 'All Shook Up' had just been released and within five days the single sold three-quarters of a million copies. The Colonel announced a nine-date, fourteen-show tour between films. Before embarking, Elvis took a train from Hollywood to Memphis where he hoped to get some rest. Instead he bought Graceland.

A New Fever

The tour opened in Chicago on March 28, 1957. The city's Catholic Interscholastic schools distributed flyers advising their students not to support Mr. Presley and his demons. The hall was subsequently packed. When Elvis appeared, he could only quell the hysteria by starting a song. The hush lasted two words, then yielded to a new fever. This was the premiere appearance of his gold lame outfit, styled by Nudie of Hollywood. It reflected the singer's exuberance, mirrored the ecstasy of his fans. Elvis was proof of youth power. He made them all kings and queens, basking in the riches of a new world.

A fifteen year old girl wearing a low-cut, fur-trimmed, and clinging piece of a dress told a Chicago reporter she'd bought the outfit hoping it would get her invited backstage. During 'Love Me Tender,' girls of all ages in the audience found themselves standing, arms outstretched, attempting to fill their embrace. A mother of three reached over her children to touch him, and tears of joy rolled down her face.

Other ballads followed 'Love Me Tender' into Elvis's repertoire, allowing him to perform sixteen songs per set, igniting Chicago for forty-seven minutes. The owner of the private ushering company, which supplied 175 of its finest alongside 100 Chicago cops and forty firemen, said he'd worked World Series games and the Kentucky Derby and no crowd had been harder to control. A Chicago wrestling promoter offered Elvis $10,000 to referee a bout the next night. But Elvis had a date in St. Louis. There, the girls of Notre Dame burned his likeness and marched in an angry processional. St. Louis sold out.

An ad from a Chicago weekly magazine: 'A man sings – and an audience goes haywire! It's Elvis Presley. The most controversial man in show business. Millions worship him. Millions would run a mile if they heard his voice.'

'Mass hysteria,' said the Detroit News, 'drowned out reports that the swivel-hipped, guitar-strumming singer is losing his hold on teenagers... An unnerving situation developed after the afternoon show, with Presley safely out of the building. His fans, refusing to believe he was gone, piled up behind police barricades about 1,000 strong and threatened to trample the police and each other in an effort to get to Presley's dressing room.'

Los Angeles Mirror-News: 'The madness reached its peak at the finish with "Hound Dog"... he got down on the floor with a huge replica of the RCA singing dog and made love to it as if it were a girl.'

Elvis arrives in Ottawa

Hello Canada

He arrived in Toronto at three AM on April 2nd, driving his personalized pink Cadillac. Despite the hour, he had to be hustled into the King Edward Hotel through a side entrance. By mid-morning, his four bodyguards were regularly hauling female fans from his door. They couldn't get to him, but someone nicked his monogrammed floormats.

In Ottawa, another Notre Dame Convent banned his show. Another sellout. A mob of sixty fans – many carrying pledges from their teachers asking that they not participate in 'Elvis activities' – besieged hotels all over the city. At this press conference, he said *Love Me Tender* 'would have done as well without me,' and later added, 'If I could become as good an actor as Frank Sinatra, I'd go into acting seriously.'

One journalist satisfied Elvis' detractors, relishing in his report that a man was beaten and robbed after the show by five leather-jacketed hoodlums. Also that eight cars were stolen, and disorderly conduct was reported on the

As usual, whisked to and from venues in a fast limousine

streets and in a nearby theater. Seven boys were jailed and two others were already out on bail. The auditorium itself was unscathed. The General Manager said, 'We are completely astonished to find that not so much as five dollars worth of damage was done.' Mexico, nonetheless, banned Elvis from the whole country.

Dropping back into the States, Elvis performed four shows over two days in Philadelphia. During 'All Shook Up,' a gang of boys in the balcony tossed an egg at his gold lame jacket, hitting Scotty Moore's guitar. Elvis finished the song, then said, 'Most of you people came here to enjoy the show. The guy who threw the egg will never make it. [Addressing the balcony] I mean it, Jack. We're just trying to put on a nice show.' A newspaper reported that the stage dust swept up after his shows would be sold to fan clubs.

On August ninth, five Pacific Northwest dates were announced. He arrived in Spokane on the Great Northern Empire Builder, whisked from the train station to the Ridpath Hotel. A Vancouver

reporter previewed that show and wrote, 'It is a frightening thing for a man to watch [Elvis'] women debase themselves.' His Canadian headline was: 'Daughter Wants To See Elvis? Kick Her in the Teeth!' Twenty two thousand Vancouver fans turned out.

Resignation

During a twenty minute layover at the train station in Havre, Montreal, 1000 fans chanted, 'We want Elvis!' The king was tired and could not oblige. They booed him. As this tour wound down, a September 27 Tupelo show was announced, a benefit for the Elvis Presley Foundation's construction of a 17-acre park and a guitar-shaped swimming pool in East Tupelo. Hollywood consumed more of Elvis' time, and one of the tolls was on his band. For two years, Scotty Moore, Bill Black, and D. J. Fontana had been on the same salary: $200 per week on the road, $100 per week off, a Christmas bonus of $1000; they had to pay their own expenses. Scotty and Bill had

Ottawa Journal, April 4, 1957: 'In gold lame, he slithered and reeled until the sweat poured from his brow and his lank hair covered his eyes. By the time 'Hound Dog' arrived for the third time round he had his audience in his hand, but not in his lap, the entourage of policemen saw to that. Then in a last pop of flashlight bulbs, he was gone. They hadn't heard his voice, but they were happy. They drowned out his every word, but his hips had kept the beat'

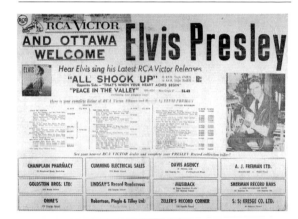

Vancouver, 9/1/57: 'A gang moved into our town to exploit 22,000 preconditioned adolescents, hired our policemen to stop anyone who wanted to get too close, then left with the loot and let the police and kids fight it out for what was left – nothing... [The show] had not even the quality of a true obscenity; merely an artificial and unhealthy exploitation of the enthusiasm of youth's body and mind. One could call it subsidized sex... Girls were punched, lifted bodily back into the heaving mass. Their escorts, teenagers like themselves, threatened the police and cadets. One bulky youth, his nose spurting blood, was hurt till he screamed. On stage, Presley winked again for his cronies to move into another wiggling song. It was obvious he was enjoying himself... Musically, one cannot say a word because of the screaming from the stage and audience.'

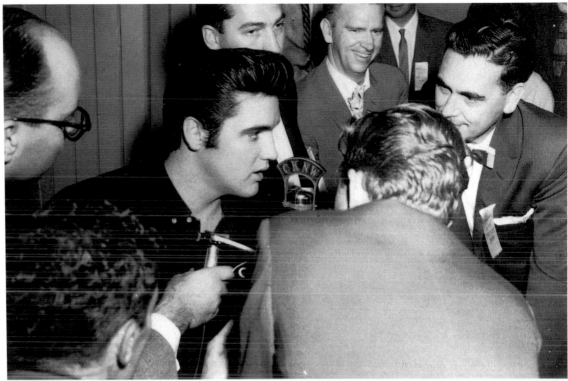

Another city, another press call

On the night of Elvis' Ottowa performance, only thirty seven members were present in the 259-member House of Commons.

been around Elvis since before anything, and while they'd seen his steady financial growth, they had watched their own finances plummet. Feeling under-appreciated and over-used, the two of them signed a letter of resignation. Scotty Moore told the Associated Press: 'Elvis is the star and we know it. I didn't expect to get rich on this, and I certainly don't begrudge him any of the success he has had or what it's brought him, but I did expect to do better than I have and to make a good living for my family.' Their resignations were effective as of several days before Tupelo. Elvis phoned them, and Scotty said they would need a modest fifty-dollar per week raise, plus $10,000 cash 'so I could clean up my debts and have something to show for these four years. Elvis said he wanted a couple of days to think it over.' Nashville session musicians backed him in Tupelo, after which Elvis and the Blue Moon Boys reunited, together until his military service.

A west coast tour followed the completion of *Jailhouse Rock*. Despite the fact that several

newspapers took some hefty critical shots at Elvis, and often below the belt at that, the public responded with sellouts.

The battle peaked in Los Angeles. After Elvis' first of two nights at the Pan Pacific Auditorium, Dick Williams, critic for the Los Angeles Mirror-News, wrote a review labelling the show a 'corruption of the innocent,' a 'lesson in pornography,' and comparing the show to 'those screeching, uninhibited party rallies which the Nazis used to hold for Hitler.' Though his descriptions applied better to Hollywood's moguls and their product, Williams's caught the attention of the LAPD. Their order was crisp: 'Clean it up and tone it down.' The next night, the cops gave Elvis their own screen test. Through hand gestures, he repeatedly indicated to the audience that their censorious camera was on him. At one point, he thrust his hands straight out, wrists together, suggesting that his actions were handcuffed. He even announced to the 9200 fans, 'You shoulda been here last night!'

Backstage during the Canadian tour

Another town, another fan club

Nearly 30,000 people saw the shows in Toronto...

... forty minutes each, sixteen songs

Though school was not out when doors for the Toronto matinee show opened, 200 young fans were there to rush in. That number swelled quickly, among it two dozen cops.

The female fans weren't necessarily teenagers

Here He Is, Teen-Agers!

WEARING HIS FAMED gold jacket, Elvis Presley walks toward the stage in Sicks' Stadium Sunday night to perform for a crowd of some 15,000 persons, mostly teen-agers. Behind Presley is part of his huge police escort. Screaming teen-agers can be seen standing up to welcome their idol. The crowd was orderly, however. This was Presley's first visit to Seattle.
—(Post-Intelligencer Photo by Eddy Manners.)

THE OREGONIAN, SUNDAY, AUGUST 18, 1957

Look And Listen:

Suits Of Armor Suggested During Presley Ticket Sales

BY JOHN VOORHEES

A suit of armor might well be the costume of the day for those who work at Sherman, Clay and Co. this Friday, for this is the day tickets for the Elvis Presley appearance go on sale there.

Presley is booked for a concert at 8:30 p. m. September 1 in Sicks' Seattle Stadium as well as concerts in Spokane (August 30), Vancouver, B. C. (August 31), Tacoma (afternoon of September 1) and Portland, (September 2).

And if all the tickets available are sold (and Zollie Volchok and Jack Engerman, who are booking the concerts, forecast they will), 118,400 people in the Pacific Northwest will have seen and heard Presley by September 3.

Mail orders have already been pouring in ever since the concert was announced and Volchok states that the first letter received was from Mrs. Carolyn Taylor, 2046-42d N. who isn't "wild" about Presley but she does have two sons who are. Mrs. Taylor, it appears, will have a front row seat whether she's a Presley fan or not.

ON STAGE—The University Playhouse's current production of "Vie Parisienne" steps aside this Friday night and the UW Opera Theater, directed by Dr. Stanley Chapple, takes over with two chamber operas, "The Old Maid and the Thief" by Menotti and Alec Wilder's "Sunday Excursion." The productions will be repeated August 17, 20 and 21 and "La Vie Parisienne" will resume August 23.

Continuing at the Penthouse is "The Chalk Garden;" the Showboat has "Lo and Behold" and the Bellevue Playbarn is presenting "Janus."

The movie reviews, which are usually found in this column on Fridays, will appear on Saturday.

The Oregonian

VOL. XCVII—NO. 30,214   PORTLAND, OREGON, TUESDAY, SEPTEMBER 3, 1957   PRICE FIVE CENTS

Hey, Kids---Here's Elvis

Labor Day Really Elvis Day

ALL SHOOK UP This is what some 14,000 real gone Presley fans saw at Multnomah stadium Monday night. Crowd was noisy, but orderly, to relief of special police retained to protect him from fans.

BACK STAGE Teen-age excited minors got chance to ask personal questions of their idol before he went on stage. They found him polite, sunshiny and direct in his answers. Mostly they asked about his love life, what he thinks about teenagers who try to maul him, when he will be drafted. (Staff photos by de Lay)

Elvis' Wild Gyrations Thrill Teen-Agers

Typical of the teen-age reactions to Elvis Presley at the stadium last night was the wide-eyed enthusiasm shown by this small segment of the crowd of 12,500 who saw the popular rock and roll singer perform.

Even the dirt Elvis Presley kneeled on was a souvenir for about 50 teen-agers who swooped down out of the grandstand for a handful as Presley left the stadium. The crowd was extremely noisy but well-behaved.

Teen-Agers Knocked Out—
Same Old Thing - Elvis Presley Wows 'Em

'Greater than ever' the banner read – and he was

'Last night' he had performed with an abandon not felt since he'd first realized his own powers. Los Angeles had become a second home to him, without the restrictions of his Bible belt residences. After rolling on the floor in his gold lame with a stuffed dog, he hosted a small party in his emerald green suite at the Beverly Wilshire, treating Sammy Davis Jr., Carol Channing, Nick Adams and others to cheeseburgers, colas, and chocolate cake. Alcohol was not permitted.

Four thousand Hawaiian fans greeted Elvis' boat when he arrived for two gigs hastily arranged after the filming of *King Creole* was postponed. Performing live was losing its appeal. His fans obliterated the music with their screams, and Elvis realized that the suggestion of himself would soon make his own presence obsolete. Instead of losing himself in his performances, he began objectifying himself, making the audience perform for him. His life had changed so blame fast. Nothing was normal anymore. When just three years earlier he'd been performing for a handful of his fellow high school kids, now he was greeted by thousands of South Pacific faces.

Kindness remained in his heart. Before he performed in Honolulu, he took time to send a note to nine year old Antoinette Mendonca, who lay paralyzed in a nearby hospital. 'Dear Antoinette, I was so sorry to hear that you are ill. Please get well, honey. I'll be thinking of you. Your Pal, Elvis.' Her parents said it was the first time her eyes expressed happiness since she'd been ill.

Farewell
Elvis' draft notice arrived on December 20th. After a farewell performance in Memphis, on March 23, 1958, Elvis opened for Uncle Sam at Fort Hood for eight straight weeks. During his two years in the service, his mother died, and rumors abounded. What was to materialise as *Aloha From Hawaii* was hinted at back in 1959, when Colonel Parker announced that he was working on a Memphis homecoming which would be broadcast to other theaters live on closed circuit television.

The Honolulu Advertiser, 11/11/57: 'The singer is obviously an expert at teasing the greatest possible hysteria from his teenage worshippers. The best example was his closing number, 'Hound Dog,' which brought the audience to its feet from the opening note. Presley threw his hips around, wobbled his knees, flopped his shoulders and shook all over until girls in the stands were hopping up and down with excitement. Then, for the first time, he sat down on the edge of the stage. Teenagers began pressing forward to see better and the police nervously closed ranks. Finally, he hopped down upon the grass in front of the stage. The crowd nearly went crazy. Girls climbed up to stand on the sides of the box I was sitting in. Others were standing precariously on their chairs. Meanwhile, Presley was rolling on the grass moaning out the words of "Hound Dog." But Elvis was not objectionable. He was loose but not lewd.'

When the mayhem died down, Elvis stepped to the microphone, felt the tension ripple through the house, ripple through his body, reverberate between himself and the crowd.

Fans Sob, Shriek As Elvis Sings For Thousands At Home Town Fair

THEY LIKE ELVIS. — These are some of the girls who went into near-hysterics while Elvis was giving his benefit performance Friday night at the Mississippi - Alabama Fair.

Another hometown date in Tupelo, 1957

Above and opposite, Tupelo 1957

A backstage escape escorted by Tupelo police

'It isn't the Memphis wriggler
who's the missing link –
it's his audiences.'

Elvis on the Sinatra show with (l to r) Joey Bishop, Frank Sinatra, Nancy Sinatra and Sammy Davis Jr

1957-61 The King of Rock'n'Roll

Discharged from the Army March 5th 1960, on the 26th Elvis guested on Frank Sinatra's TV show. Though he was a model for Elvis's acting, Ol' Blue Eyes, in 1957, had been less than courteous in the prominent magazine *Western World*: 'My only deep sorrow is the unrelenting insistence of recording and motion picture companies upon purveying the most brutal, ugly, degenerate, vicious form of expression it has been my displeasure to hear – naturally I refer to the bulk of rock and roll. It fosters almost totally negative and destructive reactions in young people. It smells phony and false. It is sung, played and written for the most part by cretinous goons and by means of its almost imbecilic reiterations and sly, lewd – in plain fact, dirty – lyrics, and as I said before, it manages to be the martial music of every sideburned delinquent on the face of the earth. This rancid-smelling aphrodisiac I deplore. But, in spite of it, the contribution of American music to the world could be said to have been one of the healthiest effects of all our contributions.'

Shorn of his sideburns, this is show-biz

Appearing in a black tux, Elvis was, as always, gracious. He closed the show in a duet with the host, blending 'Witchcraft' with 'Love Me Tender'

is who might be considered the luckiest kids in town, waited at far end of the train
able to meet Elvis Presley when he arrived in Portland Monday. They are, from left,
larx, Patty Marx, Judy Breall and Marcella Marx. They showed him small guitar and
them autograph in return before hurrying to hotel. (Staff photos by Allan de Lay)

Car Whisks Elvis Away

Additional details on page 27.

Elvis Presley — voice, hips, guitar and all—arrived in Portland Monday afternoon on a train that didn't appear to be the least "shook up."

But with the first sounds of the incoming engine that was bringing the bobby-sox hero into flesh-and-blood presence, a horde of young fans in the union depot let out shrieks and squeals that they just couldn't hold any longer.

The teen-agers had been waiting around the train station for hours Monday in the hope that he had selected that mode of transportation. His press agents had attempted to keep his arrival a deep secret.

Press Agents Win

The press agents won in the end, however. They had him whisked off the far end of the train—about a quarter of a mile from the depot lobby—and into a car before the excited worshipers knew what had happened.

Apparently resigned to the fact they would have to wait and see him at the one-night performance at Multnomah stadium, the throngs moved immediately in that direction.

By 8 p. m. some 6500 to 7000 eager fans were waiting on the edge of their seats. Many were still lingering at the entrances and the crowd total was expected to be swelled by 8:30 curtain time.

Traffic in the stadium area was, of course, a problem. Some 100 city policemen were detailed to keep the cars moving and the teen-agers settled.

Elvis responded simply. 'I admire the man. He has a right to his opinion, but I can't see him knocking it for no good reason. I admire him as a performer and an actor, but I think he's badly mistaken about this. If I remember correctly he was also part of a trend. I don't see how he can call the youth of today immoral and delinquent.' Their alliance signalled a change for Elvis, a coming to terms with hype. That episode of the *Frank Sinatra – Timex Hour* (aired on May 8th) was renamed *Frank Sinatra's Welcome Home Party for Elvis Presley,* occurring just after he'd come home. Hours before Elvis' train arrived in Miami, a bulletin alerted trains in the area to mobs of fans meandering on the tracks. When Elvis arrived, he couldn't disembark. His car reappeared on another platform, and while the decoy was mobbed, the train went to a nearby crossing, where another vehicle was waiting. Scenes at the Fountainebleau Hotel were similar. His limo was swarmed by fans, and Colonel thought it safer to keep Elvis inside. The mob was appeased by the limo.

IN
GRATEFUL APPRECIATION
TO

MISTER GREEN

FOR SERVICES RENDERED FAR IN EXCESS OF EXPECTATIONS IN
BEHALF OF THE NEEDY. THIS SERVICE IN CONJUNCTION WITH
THE MEMPHIS CHARITY SHOW -- PRESLEY 100% BENEFIT --
CONTRIBUTED GREATLY TO THE SUCCESS OF SAME, FOR WHICH
WE GIVE OUR SINCERE THANKS.

Elvis Presley
and
THE COLONEL

Memphis, Tennessee
February 25th, 1961

I n November of 1960, Elvis' first post-army live engagements were announced: two charity shows in Memphis. Then, that December, on the anniversary of the Pearl Harbor bombing, a brief editorial caught the Colonel's eye: 'Other battlefields and other heroes have been suitably remembered. But no permanent memorial stands in salute to the dead of Pearl Harbor.' Promptly, he announced a March benefit for just such a memorial.

Preparations for the shows were simultaneous. Colonel Parker set the tone when he stated of Hawaii, 'Every penny of that money taken in must go to the fund, otherwise we are not interested in doing the show.' The fund was $50,000 short, so that amount became the goal.

In Memphis, twenty-four local charities were to benefit. Media from *Variety* to the *Memphis Hebrew Watchman* hyped the show, which included a comic/impressionist, a twelve-piece band, acrobats, singer/comedian Brother Dave Gardner, the Jordanaires, and toastmaster George Jessel.

The homecoming sold out in four hours. A matinee show was added, along with three more charities to benefit.

The first ticket buyer for the charity concerts was a sixty-year-old Memphis widow

Elvis, the most famous Memphian in history, was lauded by the establishment, from the Mayor to ordinary cops, eager to perform their duty at his shows

Elvis rehearsed at Graceland the night before the show. At the luncheon, he eluded 500 fans by entering the hotel via a guarded door off the back alley, taking the service elevator to the second floor kitchen, and entering the Balinese Room through a pantry. There were speeches and ceremonies. Not long back, his brethren considered him scandalous, but on February 25, 1961, the Memphis mayor said, 'It makes me proud to say Elvis is part of our city.' RCA Records presented him with a plaque for selling seventy-five million records. That figure included the million copies of 'Surrender' which had just been released. An RCA rep was called to the phone, then announced that since the plaque had been inscribed, Elvis had sold another million records. To everything, including the standing ovation which closed the event, Elvis responded with a gracious 'Thank you'

At the press conference which followed, when asked if he was happy, Elvis replied, 'Oh, I don't know. I'm nervous...'

Robert Johnson was a writer at the Memphis Press-Scimitar, and an early supporter of Elvis. At the press conference, he asked:

Q. What will you be doing 10 years from now?
A. I'll tell you Mr. Johnson – I would not say. Everything is changing. People change. Times change. I'm trying to make it acting. It takes a long time. It takes a lot of work and experience. I don't know how long the music will last.
Q. Will you go barnstorming into the future?
A. Colonel Parker could answer that better. Eventually I'll have to do a European tour because of those people over there.
Q. Wouldn't you like to take your money and get away from the hub-bub?
A. No, I enjoy it. Any time I want to be alone I can be. Those are the type of things you have while they last. I have a pretty good time.
Q. How many cars?
A. Two – the pink car, the one my mother liked best, a Cadillac. I am going to keep it. It is the first I ever owned. I had a sports car in Germany. They can get you in a lot of trouble.
Q. What was your greatest thrill in show business?
A. I imagine it was my first gold record. I cannot pick out any one thing.

The Memphis charity shows and the USS Arizona benefit that followed would be Elvis' last live concert performances until 1969

Milestone Dates: February 1961 – Memphis Charity Shows

He never lacked control once he was on stage. At the evening show, George Jessel prostrated himself before Elvis. The crowd chanted 'Elvis! Elvis! Elvis!' for a full three minutes, a paean to the master who'd broken their chains. He performed twenty songs in forty-nine minutes, dancing with a new-found Hollywood agility. When the show was finished and 'Hound Dog' had everyone up their tree, Elvis broke with tradition and came back out on stage, blowing Memphis a kiss. Then he ducked into a waiting car. *Variety* called it 'a cuffo stint.'

With all said and done, the concert raised over $60,000. Among those who benefitted were the Crippled Children's Hospital, Goodwill, the Home for Incurables, the Jewish Community Center, Les Passes, Orange Mound Day Nursery, St. Jude Hospital Foundation, Lions School for Visually Handicapped Children, and the Salvation Army. Elvis Presley was cited by the state legislature as 'one of Memphis' most outstanding citizens.' Times had indeed changed.

Memphis Press Scimitar 2/25/61: 'G. L. Coffey, superintendent at Ellis Auditorium, was in a reminiscent mood as youngsters gathered for the matinee. He recalled Elvis as a Humes High student who sold cold drinks at Auditorium shows, and after the shows would go up on the stage, take his guitar and play, though there was no audience. Now he plays to sellout crowds at Ellis Auditorium.'

Colonel Parker devised a $100-a-plate Memphis luncheon as an additional fundraiser. The Hotel Claridge donated its Balinese room and the food. The menu was the Claridge's regular $3.50 dinner: fruit cocktail supreme, candied sweet potatoes, broccoli, a tossed salad with french dressing, and a creme de menthe parfait. The package included tickets for the evening show.

Honorary citizen or not, the Memphis fans accorded Elvis the kind of welcome he loved best

Above and right, at the USS Arizona benefit

'People change... times change... I don't know how long the music will last'

The Secretary of the Navy cordially invites you to attend the Dedication Ceremony of the U. S. S. Arizona Memorial at Pearl Harbor on Wednesday the thirtieth of May Nineteen Hundred and Sixty-Two at nine-thirty A. M.

R. S. V. P.
By the first of May

Elvis' performance fee of $150,000 was waived again a month later in Hawaii. A week before the show, the Colonel purchased radio time on Oahu's thirteen stations, giving them a half-hour tape of Elvis singing spirituals. Half of the stations immediately donated the money back into the memorial for the 1102 men entombed in the sunken battleship USS Arizona. Elvis' age, twenty-

'We got off the plane, girls were screaming...

He walked over to sign autographs...

Seventy-five policemen and 3000 fans greeted Elvis at the airport. Radio coverage of his noon arrival began at 9 AM. There were full-page welcomes in all the newspapers. King Carl Motors offered $100 tickets with the purchase of any car ranging from $295 to $2595.

six, was the average age of the men killed.

The concert began with an orchestra, followed by another featuring Polynesian-style music. There was comedy, piano music from Floyd Cramer, Boots Randolph played 'Yackety Sax,' the Jordanaires sang; *Grand Ole Opry* favorite Minnie Pearl was a special guest. Following the intermission, while Elvis' band found their places, the chairman of the Pacific War Memorial Commission was introduced, so he could introduce the Admiral of the 14th Naval District, so he could introduce Elvis. Before doing so, he read a telegram from the Secretary of the Navy: 'The generosity and public spirited zeal with which you donate your services to the Arizona Memorial fund tonight are deeply appreciated by all of us in the Navy.' The Admiral, who probably had other notions in 1956, added, 'He is a fine American. He has had many starring roles, not the least of these has been as a soldier in the U.S. Army.'

Dazzled

The 4800 Hawaiian fans were dazzled by his famous gold jacket, set off by dark blue trousers, a white shirt, and string tie. His hair was sleek on the side and sans sideburns, but sported a towering top. In the course of just under an hour, he gave them sixteen songs, including 'Lonely In The Night,' 'Buttercup,' 'A Fool Such As I,' 'Surrender,' 'Don't Be Cruel,' and 'Hound Dog.' Elvis' effort raised in excess of $62,000. The Hawaii House of Representatives formally thanked Elvis and the Colonel. Colonel Parker then sent a wire to Lyndon Johnson, Vice President of the United States, advising: 'Now more than ever we feel it proper to let you know that we are willing, able and available to serve in any way we can our country and our President in any capacity, whether it is to use our talents or help load the trucks.'

Negotiations were underway for Elvis to play open-air at the Seattle State Fair the following year for a quarter of a million dollars. Fair officials asked what provisions could be made for rain, and

Parker responded with a rain clause which gave him the right to sell plastic umbrellas for a dollar. A promoter offered $300,000 to bring Elvis to Australia. A British magazine ran a story: 'It's on at last! Elvis Presley is to visit Britain next year for one mammoth concert in aid of charity, probably at the Empire Pool, Wembley, if it can be fixed.'

Elvis' record receipts had topped $80 million, fan mail was averaging twenty thousand letters a week, he was a national institution. Hollywood, which paid him comfortably, kept his visage a theatre ticket away from anyone in the world. Despite rumors, more than seven years would pass before he returned to the performing stage.

Honolulu Advertiser, 3/27/61: 'Elvis is a musical Messiah. For his fans, he has an animal magnetism that communicates itself more strongly than any entertainer I've seen or heard, an almost dictatorial control of the audience, which he wields over his disciples even when they can't hear the lyrics.'

... I'd never seen anything like it before...

... I was just horrified... I thought...

... they were going to kill him' (Minnie Pearl)

Review in The Honolulu Advertiser 3/27/61, headlined 'Presley Fans Crash Sound Barrier Here': 'The Bloch Arena was a wonderful laboratory for the study of mass hysteria, evidenced throughout by shrieking, stomping, yelling whistling and screaming… As a onetime press agent for both Johnnie Ray and Frank Sinatra, let me say that Elvis drives his fans to a frenetic response the other reaction producers couldn't approach. In that field, he is to them as a a DC-8 is to a DC-4 prop job.'

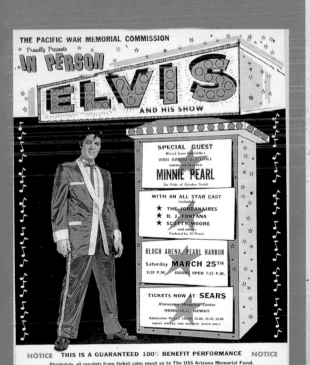

Special guest was country star Minnie Pearl, who died in 1996

'The most fascinating aspect...
is his ability to drive his fans into delirious
vocal ecstatics with a crook of his finger,
or a wiggle of his hand, a shake of his hips,
a walk across the stage, a wink of his eye.'

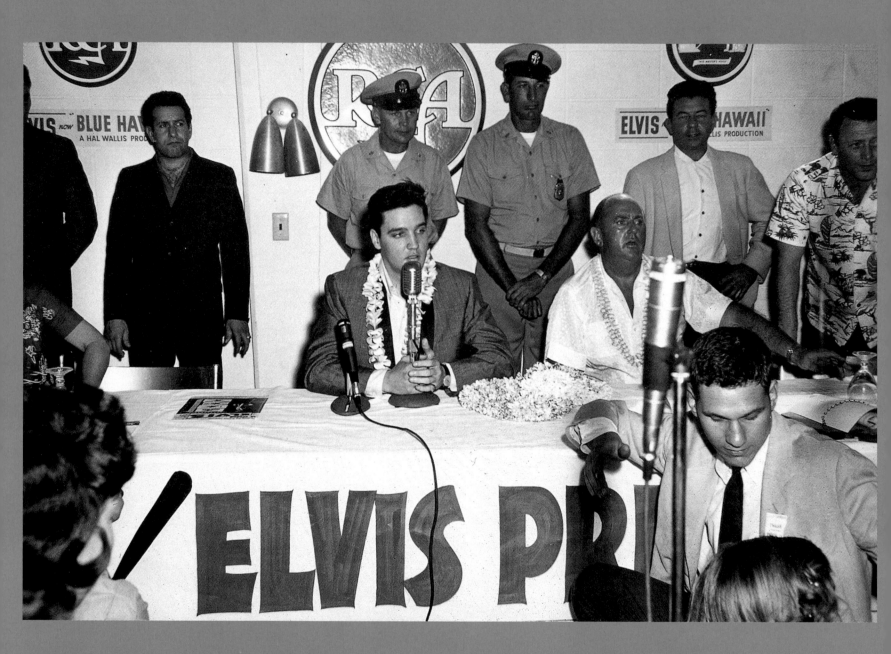

HEADQUARTERS
TRIPLER U. S. ARMY HOSPITAL
OFFICE OF THE COMMANDING GENERAL
APO 438

3 April 1961

Colonel Tom Parker
Hawaiian Village Hotel
Honolulu, Hawaii

Dear Colonel Parker:

Your kindness in purchasing expensive tickets to the Elvis Presley USS Arizona Memorial Fund Benefit for 30 of our patients is greatly appreciated.

Your thoughtfulness in remembering our patients in connection with your overwhelming generosity to the war memorial fund is most commendable and was a valued contribution to the welfare and well-being of our patients, as evidenced by their enthusiastic comments concerning the event.

As a physician, I clearly know that it takes more than the art of the doctor and the surgeon's knife to heal a sick individual and one of the important secondary aids during convalescence is good entertainment.

Thank you again for your great kindness.

Sincerely yours,

A. L. TYNES
Brigadier General, MC
Commanding

ROBERT A. EVERETT
9TH DISTRICT, TENNESSEE

HOME ADDRESS:
UNION CITY, TENNESSEE

COMMITTEE ON
HOUSE ADMINISTRATION
VETERANS' AFFAIRS

SECRETARY:
HOPE HART

Congress of the United States
House of Representatives
Washington, D. C.

March 9, 1961

Colonel Thomas A. Parker
P. O. Box 417
Madison, Tennessee

Dear Colonel Parker:

I certainly do thank you for sending me the folder describing the ELVIS show for the USS Arizona Memorial Fund.

Please allow me to congratulate you for this most worthy endeavor and to wish for you every success in your efforts. I only wish it could be possible for me to be present.

With my personal regards, I remain

Sincerely your friend,

Robert A. Everett

RECEIVED
MAR 13 1961
ALL STAR SHOWS

Accolades poured on Elvis after the Arizona show

House Resolution No. 105

THE FIRST LEGISLATURE OF THE
STATE OF HAWAII

HOUSE OF REPRESENTATIVES

Resolution

EXPRESSING GRATITUDE AND APPRECIATION TO ELVIS PRESLEY AND COLONEL TOM PARKER ON BEHALF OF ALL HAWAII FOR THEIR SERVICES IN HELPING TO RAISE THE FUNDS NEEDED FOR THE U.S.S. ARIZONA MEMORIAL.

OFFERED BY: AMANO X BAINS-JORDAN ___ BEPPU X CHANG ___ CHING ___
DELA CRUZ X DEVEREUX X DWIGHT ___ EDWARDS ___ EVENSEN ___
FERNANDES ___ FORBES X FUKUDA ___ FURTADO X GARCIA X GILL ___
HARA X HEEN ___ HENRIQUES ___ IHA X JUDD X KAMAKA ___
KATO ___ KENNEDY ___ KOGA ___ KUDO ___ KURIYAMA X LANHAM ___
LOO X McCLUNG X MEDEIROS X MIHO ___ MILLIGAN ___
MIRIKITANI X MIYAKE ___ OKANO ___ OSHIRO X PULE X
ROHLFING ___ ROSEHILL ___ SAKIMA X SERIZAWA ___ SHIGEMURA ___
SUWA ___ TAKAMINE X TERUYA ___ TRASK ___ WAKATSUKI ___
YAMASAKI ___ YEE ___ SPEAKER CRAVALHO ___

DATE OF ADOPTION: MARCH 30, 1961

We hereby certify that the foregoing House Resolution was this day adopted by the House of Representatives of the First Legislature of the State of Hawaii.

Speaker, House of Representatives

Clerk, House of Representatives

Presley Show Brings In $52,000

Elvis Presley's show played before 4,800 wildly enthusiastic persons at Bloch Arena last night and took in more than $52,000 for the USS Arizona Memorial Fund.

It even topped the $50,000 goal the rock 'n' roll star had set his sights on.

IT WAS a crackerjack show, a sellout, and the biggest single gate in the history of show business in Hawaii.

H. Tucker Gratz, chairman of the Pacific War Memorial Commission, said: "This occasion is a dream come true after 16 years. Tonight is the most important event in this effort...

"This all started when George Chaplin of The Advertiser sent a letter to newspapers across the country and a very fine gentleman read an editorial in one of the California newspapers. That man (Colonel

Tom Parker, Presley's manager) called George Chaplin and said: 'I know a young man whose services can be a big help.' "

GRATZ SAID that Parker came to Hawaii and set up the show and stipulated that every cent would go toward the War Memorial fund. "Forty-eight hours ago we met in this very room and we were $10,000 short," said Gratz. We made an agreement with Parker that he and Elvis would raise $5,000 if the War Memorial Commission would raise the other $5,000...

"I can assure you that on Dec. 7 of this year there will be a memorial."

The show was fast-paced and slick. It jumped. When Elvis came on the teenagers screamed for 2½ minutes without let-up. Elvis was wearing his famous gold jacket with the silvery glints like sequins, dark blue trousers and a white

A Gal Is Overcome By That Man, Elvis

shirt and a blue string tie.

• • •

HE WIGGLES as much as he ever did. The Army didn't make him a bit conservative.

He started singing "Lonely in the Night..." The applause was like a shock wave.

Then "Buttercup"... "Fools Such as I"..." the "big three" — "Surrender," "Don't Be Cruel," and, of course, "Houn' Dog." The applause came roaring in.

THE FIRST ACT was Phil Ingall's orchestra, a brassy combo that the audience lapped up. Soon the audience clapped along in time to the music.

Then Sterling Mossman and his group performed

Polynesian songs and launched a comedy routine that brought titters and giggles from the $100 seats. (The 300 $100 seats were just about filled. In 30 of the $100 seats sat patients and corpsmen from Tripler Army

Hospital whose tickets were paid for by Presley and Parker.)

Frank Cramer, RCA recording star, played a piano solo.

THE JORDANAIRE Quar-
See ELVIS on A-1A, Col. 5

Elvis Presley Packs 'Em in

A CROWD OF 10,419 FILLS KIEL AUDITORIUM TO CAPACITY FOR ELVIS PRESLEY SHOW

Signing and Sighing

Mingling with as many teen-agers in the crowd as possible, Elvis affably signs autographs and kisses some of his admirers. The rock 'n roll show was a complete sell-out.
—Globe-Democrat Photos by Howard Vogt and Roy Cook

Elvis Presley packs them in at Memorial Aud ... crowd was estimated at 11,000.

A Presley fan carried away by anguished enthusiasm.

Gold-Spangled Mr. Presley Wiggles For 9,000

It Was Sheer Pandemonium

THE OTTAWA CITIZEN

Riding The Elvis Special Was Weird And Wonderful!

The Police Kept It Peaceful

The 'Great Man' On Her Arm

Nobody Got Near His "Prize"

Comeback

Tubes were glowing and transistors crackled. Someone wiped a last piece of dinner from grandfather's mouth, leaned into his good ear and told him to come on in the living room, Elvis was going to do something on television. One commercial faded away. Another came on. A panicked mother raced her panicked daughter to the newspaper's TV listings, confirming yet again the right station.

I got nothing to hide. When Elvis' face filled millions of television screens the night of December 3, 1968, that was the attitude he announced. 'If you're looking for trouble/You came to the right place.' There can be no mistaking his intention now. Call it a Christmas special, call it 'The '68 Comeback,' call it 'Singer Presents Elvis.' But what is unfolding is a dare, a declaration of power, an acknowledgement of competition, and then a dismissal. It had been seven years since Elvis performed live, a dozen since he toured heavily. In that time, the Beatles had redirected the world that Elvis had created; John Fitzgerald

Kennedy, another embodiment of a new generation, had come to power and been silenced; a gradual affair with Hollywood had become a disillusioned marriage.

The celluloid years were a mixed blessing. The films were easy, sometimes fun to make, sometimes fun to watch, and always profitable. Initially, they provided a welcome relief from the stage, where concerts were having less and less to do with his performance and more and more to do with the audience's. But over the Hollywood years, a lifelessness set in. The music, which had been the original spark, became dictated by the movies. The movies, which had always been one of Elvis' goals, became dictated by easy plots. He'd quit touring when he could no longer hear himself on stage. In Hollywood, Elvis never really got to hear himself act.

Between 1961 and 1968, when he ceased performing live, only two of his records were among the top twenty-five sellers of any year: 'Return to Sender' in 1962 and 'Crying In the

Chapel,' 1965. The musical turning point began in 1966 with the first collaboration between Elvis and producer Felton Jarvis, an album of spiritual songs 'How Great Thou Art' which earned Elvis his first Grammy Award. In late '67, they returned to Elvis' blues roots and their 'Big Boss Man' broke the top forty; 'Guitar Man' and 'U.S. Male' had a new edge while recovering some of the old charm.

Landmark

On January 18, 1968, the front page of *Variety* ran a banner headline: 'Presley's 2-Ply Deal with NBC,' announcing the star's inked agreement to star in both a theatrical film and a TV special. Elvis' first post-Army press conference heralded the TV special as a landmark event. Held in an NBC-TV studio, it picked up where they'd left off, Elvis and the Colonel proving themselves as the inspiration for the wackiness of the Beatles press conferences. The entourage arrived half an hour late. Colonel led the way, followed by director Steve Binder and executive producer Bob Finkel.

When asked why he had finally yielded to TV, Parker quipped 'As you know, we have another mouth to feed next month, and we need the extra income.' Lisa Marie was born two weeks later.

There was no wide shot of Elvis in a scenic environ, no circumstance or situation whatsoever. Just Elvis Presley, full face filling screen. Right on: Elvis

The black backdrop becomes lit, revealing the ultimate expression of confidence. Within sixty seconds, Elvis has made his dominance explicit

**The lights go up to reveal a stage
filled with a hundred silhouetted
figures, some stacked four high,
each in a frame, each with a guitar,
each strutting from pose to pose.**

All those who'd coasted in his wake, who – during his absence – declared their superiority, now fell into his shadow

The floor was opened to questions, and the comedy team of Parker and Presley spun its magic. When asked why he was doing the show, Elvis said, 'We figured it was about time. Besides, I thought I'd better do it before I got too old.' Colonel Parker interrupted to add, 'We also got a very good deal.' Would Elvis be acting or singing in the special? 'I'm going to sing almost exclusively in it, and I'm going to sing the songs I'm known for.' Parker: 'If he sang the songs he's known for, that would take a couple of hours.' Has your audience changed much? 'Well, they don't move as fast as they used to'

After the special was taped and before it had aired, Elvis stirred up anticipation, telling a UPI writer, 'I'm planning a lot of changes. You can't go on doing the same thing year after year. It's been a long time since I've done anything professionally except make movies and cut albums. Before too long I'm going to make some personal appearance tours. I'll probably start out here in this country and after that play some concerts abroad,

starting in Europe. I miss the personal contact with audiences... I've already taped that Christmas show. And let me tell you my knees were shaking. Not that they were keeping time with the music. It had been just too long since I'd appeared before a live audience..'

Steve Binder, Producer/Director: 'This show is a matter of video history significance. Even if he tries, Elvis can never do another one like this one. It's introducing a great talent, at a particular stage in his development, to a whole new world that has never seen an Elvis Presley like this before. Presley is one in a lifetime. We had Joe Louis in the boxing ring and we had Manolete in the bull ring. In his area, Presley is the champ.'

'it gave me a new life. I was human again'

'There was hope for the future... it wasn't the same old movies, the same type of songs...'

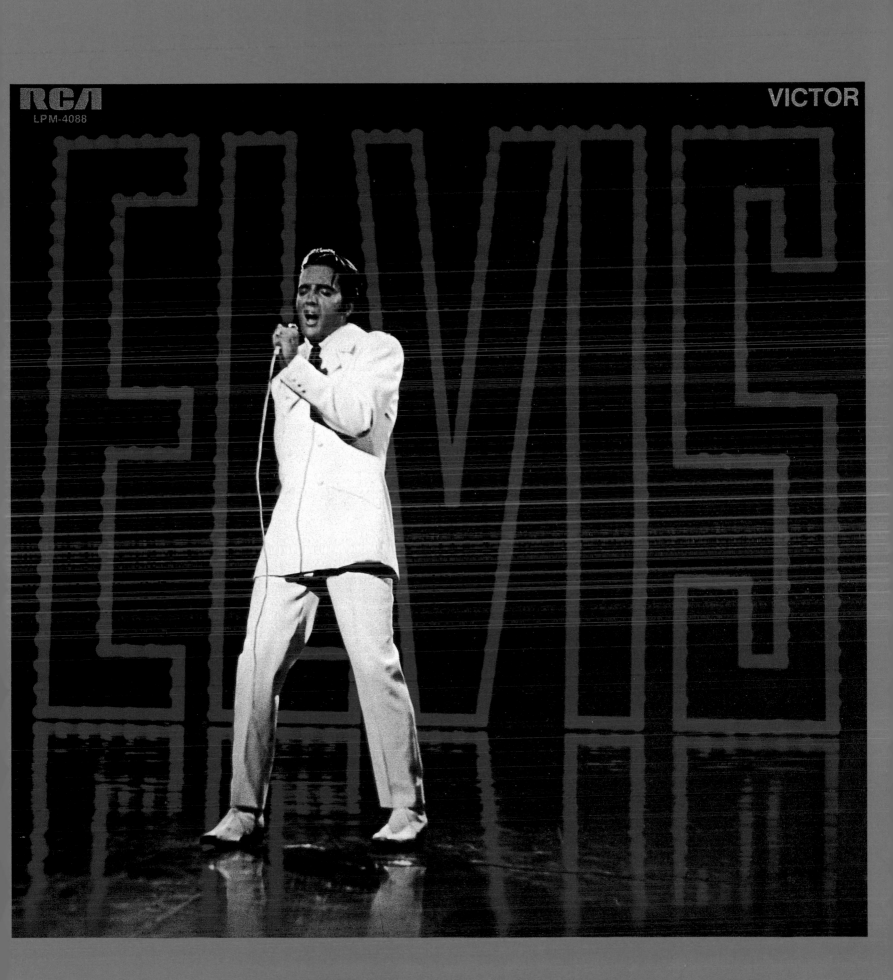

Elvis proves he is beyond imitation

There is no balance to his equation

He is singular...

... and he is back

'How many times can you sing about girls, Army days, things like that? Every picture there'd be ten or twelve songs with the best coming out as a single. There was no way they could all be good.'

'I was able to give some feeling, put some expression into my own work'

Sponsored by the sewing machine company, *Singer Presents Elvis* premiered as an NBC colorcast on December 3, 1968, from 9-10 PM eastern time. He had twenty-eight film releases to his name, but this was the first TV show he could call his own. The camera pulls back to reveal the artist in rebellious black, a blood-red scarf, a guitar hanging from his neck. His looks are stunning, his sensuality aglow. The audience of doubters – completely justified in their skepticism – could feel their pulse quickening.

After the opening scene, Elvis sits comfortably with several old friends and bandmates – among them guitarists Scotty Moore and Charlie Hodge, and drummer D. J. Fontana, the latter beating on a guitar case – running through old songs, blues classics, and hits of his own. (Bill Black had passed away in 1965.) It does not appear to be anyone's front porch, but the musicians seem unaware of that. They seem unaware of even the audience, which is spilling onto the stage right next to them. They are playing for themselves,

'It gave me a chance to do what I do best: sing...   ... I can sing what I feel now'

Milestone Dates: December 3rd, 1968 – 'The '68 Comeback'

with a heart and soul and energy that, to this day, leaps off the screen. The old power, in a new age, in a new era.

These great performances are punctuated by songs set to choreographed skits, showcasing the bevy of typically long-legged sixties beauties – clad ever so scantily – along with a few dance-cum-fight sequences in case someone didn't get enough from his movies. 'Guitar Man' threads its way through the show, a verse here and there to link a *West Side Story* idea to an Egyptian fantasy.

Reprising 'Trouble' at the close of the show, Elvis is seen – without missing a beat – in the show's many scenarios, making disjointed cuts smooth, proving that really, Elvis is everywhere. Elvis *is* everything.

The final song is the impassioned performance of 'If I Can Dream,' Elvis in angelic white, the blood red scarf. Finished, he raises his arms triumpantly, says 'Thank you, good night,' and then the camera holds on him, a medium long shot, arms fallen to his side, humble.

The special was taped before a live audience over June 27th and 29th at NBC Studio 4, Burbank.

The soundtrack album made No 8 in the *Billboard* chart, the single of 'If I Can Dream' No 12

Milestone Dates: December 3rd, 1968 – 'The '68 Comeback'

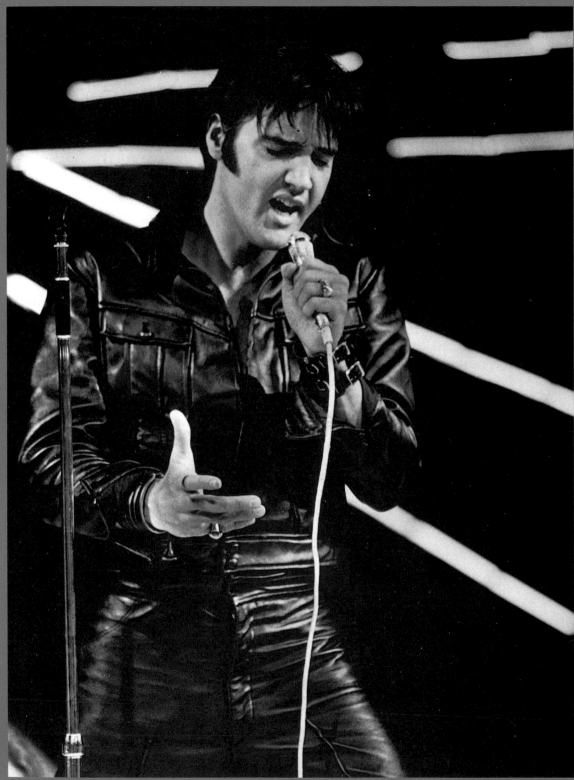

With a 32 audience rating and 42 share, 'Elvis' was the highest-rated program for the week

More women age 18 to 49 watched his TV special than any other in '68

According to Advertising Age, Network TV Program Popularity Poll, January 13, 1969.

See "SINGER presents ELVIS" Sunday Night, August 17th, on NBC-TV in Color!

A repeat airing was broadcast August 17th 1969

The 'Comeback' special was shown on British television on December 31st 1968, minus commercial breaks!

A heap of new offers followed. The London Palladium wanted an Elvis spectacular. Phoning Colonel Parker, they offered him $28,000 for the week. 'That's fine for me,' said Parker. 'Now how much can you get for Elvis?'

Finally, in May of 1969, the brand new International Hotel in Las Vegas announced that it had confirmed Elvis' first 'cafe date' in thirteen years. He was slated for a month beginning July 31, following Barbra Streisand, who opened the new venue. Hollywood had dressed up Elvis like a series of store mannequins, giving him maximum visibility with a minimum of contact.

Rehearsal

Elvis arrived in Vegas a week before his show. Daily rehearsals were strenuous. Two hours before his first curtain, he was still on stage, running through material with the band. Booked for four weeks, two shows a night, at a reported $100,000 per week, he could reach 100,000 fans. By the time the show opened, eighty percent of the whole engagement's seats were booked, one of the biggest advance reservations in Vegas history. The souvenir reservoir included more than 150,000 facsimile-autographed 8 X 10 color glossies, half a million calendars, and 200,000 catalogs listing songs, records, movies and tapes.

Panache

More than a few people were only too eager to recall Elvis' last Vegas engagement, creating a shadow from which the star would have to step. All these concerns were especially high on opening night, when the outcome was anybody's guess. While the audience was sipping Manhattans and pondering such issues, the Sweet Inspirations had the unenviable job of cutting the tension and injecting some warmth and life into the room. A quartet of black females who were also part of the featured act, their gospel vocals were an important element in Elvis'presentation, mixing down-home sincerity with Vegas panache.

Among the 2000 attending the opening were George Hamilton with Alana Collins, Burt Bachrach and Angie Dickinson, and Carol Channing with her husband Charles Lowe. Petula Clark was there, before dashing off to Caesar's Palace to do her own show, which included a favorable review of what she'd just seen. Ed Ames, who was performing at the Riviera, reported likewise. Family and old friends also came to give Elvis support, and he breathed a little easier when he thought of Priscilla in the audience, his father, his latest producer Felton Jarvis, his original producer and earliest mentor Sam Phillips, and his semi-nephews, Sam's sons Knox and Jerry.

The relief from the opening acts and the natural effects of the alcoholic drinks were sucked into a vacuum when the lights finally went down. With the moment upon them, the audience considered who and what they were about to witness, his impact on society, his hit songs, his hit films, his voice, his manner, his touch. They thought about the world they'd known before

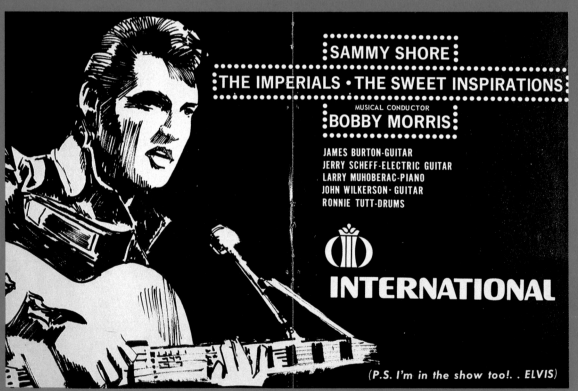

Colonel flooded radio and TV with more than 100 ads daily, and reserved full pages in the Vegas papers

Elvis' invite to Nancy Sinatra's opener

Elvis, light years gone, and the world they lived in now – the differences they'd seen which could be attributed to the Southern boy who shook his hips. They thought about the lovers they'd met while hearing an Elvis Presley song, the soundtracks he'd provided for kisses, for driving in the car, for basement parties and now for mansion parties. They thought about how much they liked this man, this ordinary man like them who was so extra-ordinary, so special, so magical. And there he was.

There had been a stage and a gold lame curtain, and now there was Elvis Presley.

And who is doing that screaming? Is it me?! He came out grinning. Dressed in a black karate-inspired two piece outfit, physically fit and trim, his hair dry where it had been slick, fuller and with more prominent – and contemporary – sideburns, he strapped on his acoustic guitar, thought about Scotty Moore and Bill Black and the Overton Park Shell so many years ago, laughed a little to himself, maybe turned around to see that the band was really behind him and to confirm that all this was really happening, and then in a flash, he began doing what he did best.

Welcome

'Well it's one for the money...' And the audience roared approval for the next hour, welcoming Elvis back to live performing, back to the Vegas that had not been so welcoming before, back to the stage and the audience and the lights and the sweat and especially, most especially, the roars and screams of happy fans.

His mike in one hand, he directed the show with his other, putting emphasis where he wanted it, restraining the musicians when he desired a softer effect.

The women screamed like they had in the past – uncontrollably – and he pandered to them, giving scarves from around his neck, kissing a few, shaking many hands. Hearty approval after hearty approval, his audience gave not one but two standing ovations.

Selections from Vegas set: Blue Suede Shoes, I Got A Woman, Love Me Tender, Jailhouse Rock, Don't Be Cruel, Heartbreak Hotel, All Shook Up, Hound Dog, Memories, In the Ghetto, Yesterday, Hey Jude, One Night, Johnny B. Goode, Suspicious Minds.

The RSVP on the opening night private invitation included the option: 'I will... be accompanied by my lady.'

The return to live performing rejuvenated Elvis. In the showroom alone, Elvis generated over a million and a half dollars in revenues. Vegas was filled with tears of happiness, tears of joy, tears for Elvis, tears for money. Money for Vegas, money for Elvis, memories for the fans. Elvis. Elvis. Elvis.

Possibilities

One screaming headline shortly after his return read, 'Elvis Rejects $5 Million Bid.' The offer was a contract for four weeks a year for the next ten years at an unnamed Vegas hotel. But Elvis did not need such long range commitments. With the success of his comeback, the future was boundless. Stating as much, Elvis and the Colonel took out full page ads on Sunday, August 17, before their run was concluded. Showing Elvis from the '68 TV special, proud and proper in his black leather suit, the message managed to be humble and ironic: 'Thanks a million, Elvis and the Colonel.' That same day, Singer had full page ads, offering congratulations for their successful return, and encouraging viewers to tune in to the rerun of *Singer Presents Elvis* at nine that night.

The first intimation of Elvis' future plans were announced on October 23, 1969, when Houston and the world learned he would play six shows at the Astrodome, February 27, 28 and March 1 of the coming year, as part of the 38th annual edition of the Houston Livestock Show and Rodeo. Before that, another month in Vegas.

Crossroads

In Vegas, he again entered unannounced, himself a little calmer this time, even if his audience was nearly as uproarious. And he tore into an old hit, 'All Shook Up.' The main difference between the opening night of the new show and of his last one – besides having Ringo Starr in this audience – was that four times during this show, he brilliantly forgot words to songs. It gave him life like nothing in Hollywood could ever produce. The humanity of it all! The blood coursing through his veins, the audience's stunned pause, then even more stunning realization: Elvis! So human! He handled each flub gracefully, so much so that they could not be called 'flubs,' but rather life-affirming moments, career-affirming moments. Coming off the plastic, silver, and deceit of light which is the movie industry, back into the real world – Las Vegas as the gateway to Houston. By forgetting his lines he was inviting every single person in the audience to share the stage with him, to confirm the American dream. Hey, don't look at me folks, I'm just a guy who got lucky, and the mountain that I'm on top of, it's not *my* mountain, it's *our* mountain, a mountain we made together. The crossroads where Robert Johnson met the devil, the rock where Moses stood, Muhammed's camel, fishes and loaves and Elvis.

Vegas opened January 26 and ended on February 23. Houston began four days later. He was ready for Houston, and the road beyond. 'I'm sick of this [dressing] room,' he told a reporter 'All I've seen since opening night is this room, the kitchen hallway, an elevator and my bed.'

His set was a mix of old and new hits...

A few songs borrowed, a blues or two...

'He was, and remains, most important of all...'

'When I work with a live audience, I can see and hear their response and I feel more like myself'

While venting his frustration, he took a shot at Hollywood, where he was still active, where he still yearned for a role outside his cookie cutter, a role with depth. 'We're looking all the time. I want a good property to find out if I can or can't act once and for all. Those others were nothing, but finding something good is hard. Everyone is buying good things and producing them themselves. I need something good. I just can't go back to girls and GIs and things like that.'

Houston sealed the comeback. When tickets went on sale by mail order, requests came in at nine hundred per day. Fans had made three singles gold since his comeback, three of his albums too. Everyone knew that the people had not forgotten, but they had not been tested. And now they passed, colors flying. The Houston audience responded exactly as Elvis needed, exactly as the Colonel knew. They were impatiently patient through the Sweet Inspirations, through Sammy Shore, the Imperials, Joe Guercio and his orchestra. It was the Vegas show (Glenn Hardin

Elvis International Times, June 1970, issue #2, 'Vegas Revisited' by Maria Luisa Davies: 'The waiting in line for Elvis' shows was no different from before. If you wanted to get down in front you had to be in the front of the line with a roll of money in your hand. Wednesday 18th February we were due to see the Dinner Show at 8 PM so we took our place in the line at 4:30 PM... When the time came to go into the Showroom I followed the same drill as before and tipped the waiter 20 dollars. I was appalled to be seated third table from the side of the room and about the 10th and 11th seat up from the stage. I told him I refused to accept the seats... Then he came back and moved us to the very centre table, and the 5th and 6th seat up from the stage. We were overjoyed because there within stretching distance was the mike, and we would have an uninterrupted full length view of Elvis... [Finally] there he was, unassuming and unannounced. He wore a pale blue jump suit with a white scarf and white sash. The outfit was in one

piece. It zipped up the front to just about the third rib and then was open to the neck, and had the stand up collar. The collar and the opening to the waist was embroidered in white with crystals, the sleeves flared at the wrist and it was trimmed with two covered buttons which were unfastened. The sash was white cord, plaited into a band about two-and-a-half inches deep and tied obliquely across his hips with the ends hanging almost to the floor. The cords, which were all loose and weighted with crystals and beads.'

Elvis was everywhere, but only by proxy. To see the real thing, you had to see the show.

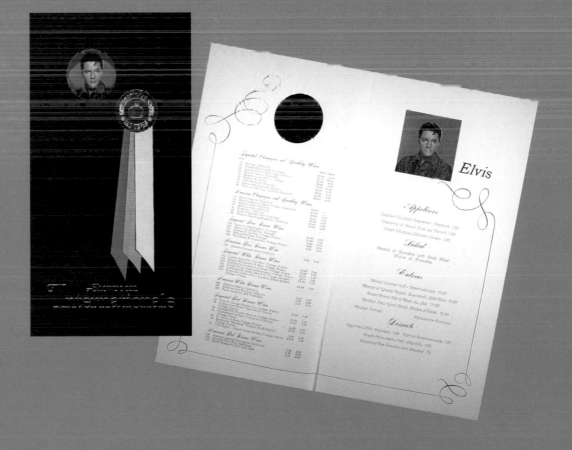

now on the piano), but in a larger venue, without dinner, without tables. It was the Vegas show, but it was altogether different.

A wave, a greeting, maybe a joke. Then: 'All Shook Up.' Indeed.

And in case things got out of hand, the good old pick was set: Forty cops lined the stage as protection. At the Saturday matinee show, there was a tense moment when a young man snuck through the rodeo chutes, eluding the barrier of policemen, and made his way toward Elvis' stage. His intent was unclear, but there was something vaguely menacing about it, something surreal, a single small fan crossing that vast and huge field, one step at a time. The police tackled him and he was removed with hardly an interruption.

Striking Out

Elvis reached over 200,000 fans in his three days, breaking attendance records at the annual event. He treated the huge venue the way he treated all venues: like he owned the stage, like he invented it. He didn't play to mobs, he played to individuals. He was loose and having fun, moving about wildly when he felt like it, then – if he so desired – he soul sang his way down to the floor, lay on his back, knees up like he was watching TV at home. He returned to Vegas that summer of 1970 before striking out on an extended tour, his first since 1957. Everywhere he went, the house came tumbling down.

There's a picture of him on stage, lying on the floor, a grown man of thirty-five caught rolling around. 'This is one of the photos that get into your blood!' a fan wrote in the *Elvis International Times*. 'It's the height of pure frenzy, the end of an enthralling show, the crown of Elvis' immortality. How can there be people who ask and wonder how long Elvis will last? They have not understood that Elvis is not only a singer, is not only Elvis; he is a feeling, part of our life and part of our youth. Who has the courage to throw away so many hours spent together with his voice, who has the courage to throw away his own youth?'

A lady booked two shows a night for five nights

No longer the hip-swiveller of his youth...

Instead, the precision of the karate he studied...

That did not prevent him from poking fun at his old self, bending the microphone low to the ground, like the soul singers he'd seen on Beale Street

Superstar

Elvis didn't sing in the decade of the seventies, he happened to it. From exile on Hollywood Boulevard, he delivered himself to his fans, reaching out to them, their city's largest auditorium, twice nightly in Vegas, a month at a stretch. Gone so long, and so many songs to sing, so many stages to climb, so many fans to whip into a frenzy. His caped arms spread wide, the man becomes a sunset, a winged creature, a vision: Past. Present. Future.

Whether opening with 'That's All Right' or 'C. C. Rider,' Elvis immediately reminded his thirsty followers that he was but the messenger, the vessel. You'll remember this one, we were kids then, we couldn't be contained by the black and gray world of our parents, by their crew cuts and societal shackles. We wanted the colored lights, we wanted electric guitars, we wanted out of the box: me and you. Me, Elvis Aaron Presley, and you (insert your name here), and now we've got it. Sharing. I'm up on stage and you're paying to see it, but it's a give and take, it's communal. I wouldn't be here if it weren't for you and you wouldn't be here if it weren't for me, and it's too hideous a thought to even consider where we'd be if we hadn't changed the world, blue lights, if we hadn't broken the bonds, red lights, if our salvation had not come in rock'n'roll, strobe lights, freedom, liberation, individualism, bellbottoms, jumpsuits, flares, puffs, embroidery,… and Elvis.

American Trilogy
'Love Me Tender,' 'All Shook Up,' another song please. Another scarf for the audience. What are the women screaming for? Why are the men so rapt? It's like the old days, but it's so plainly not like the old days. Elvis remains Elvis, but the world has become Elvis, all music is Elvis. Let's party in Las Vegas, let's glitz it up, turn the lights on so bright that night never comes around, that fear is no more a part of us than crapping out at the dice table. Me and you, we're all winners. We are all part of the American Trilogy, black and white, blues and country, gospel quartets and rafter-shaking gospel refrains. I spread my cape, I take you all in, I offer you all of me. We are one.

After Houston, Elvis returned to Vegas, then geared up for his first full-fledged tour in a decade. September 9, 1970, hello Phoenix. 'Jerry,' a voice on the other end of the morning phone call said to concert promoter Jerry Weintraub, 'this may be the happiest day of your life. I think you ought to fly up here to Las Vegas. I want to talk to you about doing some dates with Elvis.' Concert promoter Jerry Weintraub was one among many who had made overtures to Colonel Parker about booking Elvis. For years, for one-nighters, for thousands, for millions. But that unexpected call set the old machine to grinding again.

At Colonel Parker's insistence, admission tickets were kept to a ten dollar maximum. They could have charged more, fifteen would have been easy, but ten was more democratic, allowed for a broader fan base, practically assuring a full house, while depriving no one of a paycheck.

Elvis roves the stage, end to end…

Not pacing like a tiger in a cage…

But like a man a little restless…

When he finally entered, he was never announced. He just appeared on the stage to the theme from '2001: A Space Odyssey'.

... looking for something he can't find, his scarf is a divining rod – here's one, who's on the other end?

'The audience will be attacked with the kind of showmanship that puts the magic and mystique in show business'

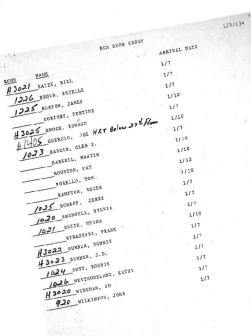

1970-77 Superstar

There was a minor problem at that first show when someone phoned in a bomb scare, turning the pressure-cooked box office into a scene of overwrought mania. But there was no stopping Elvis, and when he bounded on stage, part folk hero, part glamor defined, part preacher, part transgressor, his reception was one long roar, a deafening response emphasized by blinding flashbulbs, a response that would be echoed until he breathed his last. He strapped on his acoustic guitar, stretched out his arms to get comfortable, and in the pause before he began, before the first notes of that first recording were replayed, stage fright took flight, and everything was okay.

Phoenix was filmed, used in the opening of MGM's documentary, Elvis That's The Way It Is. An amazingly prescient film, it captures the fans, the showman, Las Vegas (where most of it was shot in the summer of 1970) and the return to touring, to life on the road – it represented a volcanic period in Elvis Presley's career. The documentation ends, and the road unfolds.

Elvis' original fans had become parents, but remained loyal to their King. Even their parents had come to admire his rich baritone, the drama in his presentation. And now there were even some new fourteen year olds, delirious gleams in a 1956 eye, making three generations of fans. In Detroit, the biggest shock was the line of ticket-buyers, orderly all day, a thousand at a time in line, patient, quiet, middle-class and straight. My my my, times do change.

The second tour became seven cities on the west coast, including two shows at the Inglewood Forum in Los Angeles. The night show there sold out – 18,700 tickets – in ten hours.

Arizona Republic Magazine 10/18/70 : 'On stage, he still exudes sex, sin, stolen pleasures. Audiences continue to be dazzled by his body – wide shoulders tapering to a slim waist, long sideburns almost to the jaw, wild, unruly hair hanging in his face, the twists, the turns, the bumps and grinds. When he loosened his green scarf and tossed it away, there were screams of delight. When he tugged at the laces of his shirt, girls and women cheered... He appeared a little bored and tired about the whole thing. He stopped singing one song. 'I don't sound very good on that one tonight,' he said. Another song bombed and Presley knew it. 'That was supposed to be sung seriously,' he said to his accompanists... From the balcony, Elvis resembled in his white costume a middle-age tennis player, a karate student and a physician on TV's Marcus Welby, M.D.'

Jumpsuits became his garment of choice...

Sometimes open to his chest, a macho man

Above and right, in action at the Houston Astrodome, 1970

Elvis greets a front-of-house salesperson vending Presley merchandise

A letter to Hilton hotel managers from Mr Barron Hilton: 'While on tour, Elvis will be doing promotional work for all Hilton hotels... it would be greatly appreciated if these items could be prominently displayed in your lobby.'

Hollywood seldom gave Elvis a proper script, but the man knew drama. He moved quickly, suddenly stopping, throwing a karate kick and standing stock still while the the music and the musicians and the audience and their thoughts and their dreams took off all around him.

Hotels were given highly detailed security precautions, sometimes running to five pages, specifying what personnel would be required for the entertainer's safety, what rooms – how many floors – would be needed, when Elvis would check in, what to do about his baggage. Off-duty cops guarded elevators with magic lists; if your name was not on it, uh uh buddy. One hotel operator said, 'All we do is meet a representative at the airport and hand them seventy-eight keys. The rest is up to them. They have their own security force, and we'll take extra precautions too. We'll never see Elvis himself, and with luck, nobody else will, either.'

Transportation in each city demanded three limos with drivers, a twenty-foot truck with driver, and a thirty passenger bus with driver – all on twenty-four hour standby. For press, the Colonel always bought time on a slew of local radio stations, showing no favoritism. No one received complimentary tickets, not even himself and Elvis.3 He gave no bios or publicity pictures to the press, allowed no tradeouts of tickets for advertising, and stipulated that the front five rows could not be held for special purchasers. Elvis had rarely granted an interview in fifteen years, and there was no reason to start. When his appearance in one city was rumored, it generated more interest than any show the promoter had confirmed. Another local promoter remarked: 'The Colonel told me that if everything goes right, I can handle Elvis here anytime he decides to come again. If anything goes wrong, he said I'd never see him again.'

Sales Pitch
In the smaller towns, Colonel Parker sometimes gathered the thirty or fifty security officers and marched them around the hall, marking an X on the floor where each was to stand. An Auditorium spokesman in Miami said that security was tighter for Elvis than it had been when President Nixon was nominated there at the Republican National Convention.

Concerts began with an announcer who reminded fans of other ways they could enjoy Elvis: his current on-tour movie, 8 X 10's which cost a mere buck, binoculars for two dollars, programs for the same. Posters, at three dollars, often sold out by intermission, so hurry. Hawking these wares was not a simple act, nor was it treated lightly. The announcer was so proficient at his task, he was often reviewed by the critics. One wrote of his 'rapid-fire sales pitch that squeezed into sixty seconds' plugs for Elvis' latest film, album, and two singles.

Jerry Weintraub: 'Everyone has to pay. That's the Colonel's orders. He pays. Presley pays. I even have to pay for my wife's ticket.' Once, Weintraub was in Colonel Parker's office when Elvis called to reserve twenty-five tickets. The Colonel responded, 'Do you want $10, $7.50, or $5 tickets?'

'He has lost none of his sexual, feline grace...'

These shows were steamrolling the way for superstardom, posing the logistical problems that kept audio engineers and equipment designers awake at night: Elvis took huge entourages into venues not previously used for such. On stage, their rocking, dancing party might number over thirty: the Joe Guercio Orchestra, the rock sextet, the three Sweet Inspirations plus one Kathy Westmoreland or Millie Kirkham for the high notes, the five gospel-singing Stamps, the Imperials or Voice. And Elvis. Sometimes the orchestras were too loud, or so many microphones created feedback problems.

When Elvis would finally enter, after the Sweet Inspirations sang 'Little Green Apples' or 'Something,' later pulling out 'Papa Was A Rolling Stone' and 'Love Train,' after the Vegas/Borscht comedy of Sammy Shore or Jackie Kahane, after more announcements about souvenirs – he simply strolled onto stage.

In 1970, the grease was gone from his hair, now blow-dried and thick, inviting to the fans'

A studio rehearsal for the Summer '70 Vegas shows, and (right) hand-written set lists for the band

fingers. His triangular sideburns were huge, and would have been a parody of his earlier trim were they not so fashionable at the time. In Vegas, he performed against a solid background, the stage bare but for the musicians that adorned it, and often they were just silhouetted. The backdrop changed colors, solids to solids, becoming a sunset, an ocean, contoured canvasses upon which the master created.

Elvis' collars were exagerrated, creating crevices of light, a dance of color augmented by the glistening studs and jewels which covered his clothes and which he wore on his fingers, his wrists, his neck. His outfits changed with the lighting, absorbing the colors the way he absorbed the dreams and emotions of his fans. His stage movements were no longer the whirling dervish of the teenage kid, but they slyly suggested it. His karate expertise created an angularity to his moves, his arms accenting the beat so that the music seemed to go through him, not like he made the movements but the movements made him.

A Leading Light

He kept time with his left leg, directing with his arms, his left hand holding the mike and flashing a big diamond ring – rings – sometimes a horseshoe of diamonds, his hand held up and keeping the luck in, held down and letting it pour out. Joe Guercio may have led the orchestra, but Elvis directed the show. He determined the accents, elongated endings, leading not just with his arms but with his whole body. His face was golden, his whole countenance was golden, beaming a special light, exuding an aura, radiant.

When he was a kid singing on stage, Elvis was a human singing his heart out, letting his soul touch his audiences. Later, though he carried the light, he was also shielded. He is Elvis Presley and he is also Elvis Presley Enterprises, and we've got lots of shows to do folks, some tonight and some more tomorrow night and some forever after, and I'm glad to be here but there also has to be some of me here tomorrow night. In the old days, he was ready to die on stage. Now, he lives every night.

Detroit Free Press, 1/31/71, Robert Kaiser after observing a rehearsal for MGM's 'Elvis – That's the Way It Is'. The song in question is the ending for 'Just Can't Help Believing':' "Tell ya what we can do," Elvis Presley says. "Let's shorten that last part. 'I just can't help believin'." He sings this four times, in a whisper, facing his backup voices. "The voices will do it four times, then the guitar will fuzz it: da da dum da!" All of them go through the ending together. Toward the end, Elvis' hand signals modulate the excessive zeal of the Sweet Inspirations until the four are almost purring.'

Rehearsals on stage at the International Hotel . .

... for the Las Vegas Summer 1970 season

'Hound Dog' was not really suited to so many instruments. If the guitar were a harmonica, if the orchestra were the audience – but Elvis turns it into fun because the fans would be disappointed without it. The ad-libbing became an outlet – on one knee during 'Suspicious Minds': 'I hope this suit don't tear up, baby.' His reassurances to the audience were also to himself, stating over and over that he was on stage for the audience's enjoyment, that his pleasure depended totally on their pleasure. A case of I hope it's as good for you as it is for me.

Repertoire

Elvis had always performed cover songs, and as his audience expanded, so did his repertoire. He turned up the juice on Credence Clearwater's 'Proud Mary,' played heartstrings like a violin on 'Funny How Time Slips Away,' put his own spin on Neil Diamond's 'Sweet Caroline,' satisfied his country yen with 'There Goes My Everything' and 'Make the World Go Away.' Politics was not a part of his show, and he dropped 'In The Ghetto' from his live set. But once, in Miami, goofing around he donned a policeman's hat, and play-acting 'the Man', he frisked the Sweet Inspirations.

Humor remained a big part of the Rock 'n Ruler's show: He introduced guitarist James Burton as Chuck Berry, pianist Glen Hardin as Jerry lee Lewis. Between songs or between lines, reaching for some water, he would suddenly toss it on his band, keeping them on their toes. His 1970s shows regularly included poking fun at his competition. 'Last time I was here,' he said in cities he hadn't visited in a decade and a half, 'I was doing then what Tom Jones has just learned to do.' His other targets were Glen Campbell, whom he imitated by singing in a very high voice, and Engelbert Humperdinck, whose smarminess made him a sitting duck. Elvis stated, 'I've sold over 200,000,000 records, and I've got fifty-six gold records. That's a record and I'm proud of it. That is more than the Beatles, Stones, and Tom Jones put together, so pfft.'

12/23/71 Jon Landau, Rolling Stone: 'After several of his recent hits, he hit his stride again in an absolutely stunning performance of 'Bridge Over Troubled Water,' which is in and of itself sufficient justification for attending a Presley performance. After finishing over an incredible climax which features every member of the troupe wailing at full blast, he lets the ovation start to build and then goes back into the last verse and does the climax again. He sings like an angel and moves like a ballerina, and he left me struck dumb.'

'His back arches...

his pelvis quivers, his left leg shakes...

his whole frame is a taut bowstring'

Elvis shares a tender moment with his wife, Priscilla

Lake Tahoe naturally flowed from Las Vegas. By 1971, Elvis was commanding $200,000 per week in Vegas, and had the Imperial Suite on the thirtieth floor. Tahoe's first two week Elvis Summer Festival sold out every engagement. The bill still featured the Sweet Inspirations and the Imperials, introducing Nipsey Russell as the comedian.

On his next tour, November 1971, Elvis returned to Houston, where the Colonel would not book him back into the Astrodome; by changing the venue when Elvis returned to a city, the Colonel could entice fans for another look. This tour introduced J. D. Sumner and the Stamps, and comedian Jackie Kahane replaced Sammy Shore. Elvis was a longtime fan of J. D. Sumner's, who claimed to be the world's lowest bass singer. Sumner was managing the Stamps when Elvis hired them, but he returned to the stage at Elvis' request. Many nights after a show, they would congregate in Elvis' suite, singing the Stamps' 'There's Something About That Name,' or other gospel favorites.

A small piece in a 1971 London daily ran the headline 'Elvis Presley Plans First British Tour.'

For the opening of Elvis' sixth stint in Las Vegas (January 26, 1972), the International printed invitations on blue felt banners, suitable for hanging in your home. The Hollywood Reporter wrote that Elvis was 'absolutely bursting with vitality, charm, and flamboyant doses of talent as singer, actor, and entertainer.' 'Elvis Now' was the theme, the name of his then-current album and a brief, fitting summation of the orbit he was the center of.

Presence

Colonel Parker was generating more and more income through various endorsements and merchandising commodities. Elvis' fine form, captured in MGM's Elvis On Tour, dispelled rumors of drug use which were surfacing in the press. In Detroit on April 7, during 'The American Trilogy,' a blue suede loafer was hurled through the air, landing within inches of his feet. Elvis never

flinched. In Richmond, a girl leapt on stage to wipe his brow and, before departing, she nicked his scarf. In San Antonio, on a later tour, one woman bit another in a fight over scarves. Elvis took it all with humor. He tried to address his fans but was usually interrupted, so he'd just start a new song. It wasn't his singing that counted, it was his presence; it wasn't his presence that counted, it was the idea of his presence.

In April of 1972, he tested his Tennessee reception in Knoxville, not yet ready for Memphis. The patient were rewarded, and even New York City got its due. June 9th was marked by a brief press conference. Wearing a pale blue suit with a long flowing, dark blue cape and a wide gold belt, the star was calm and humorous. 'Man, I was tame compared to what they do now,' he told reporters, referring to the contemporary hard rock scene. 'I didn't do anything but jiggle a little.' Asked why he's still a box office draw in concert, he replied, 'I take vitamin E. I enjoy the business. I like what I'm doing.'

ELVIS
Summer Festival
SAHARA TAHOE

Menu

Choice of One:

CRENSHAW MELON

CHILLED TOMATO JUICE

CHOPPED CHICKEN LIVERS

ICED VICHYSSOISE

FRENCH ONION SOUP AU CROUTON

CREAM OF ASPARAGUS ARGENTEUIL

CELERY VICTOR MIMOSA

GARDEN MIXED GREEN SALAD

Dressings:
Sahara's Famous Caesar, Roquefort, Creamed French,
Thousand Island, Green Goddess

**Complete Elvis Souvenir Photo Album on Sale at
Hotel and High Sierra Theatre entrance.**

Entrees

CHARCOAL BROILED NEW YORK CUT STEAK
MAITRE D'HOTEL

ROAST PRIME RIB OF BEEF
HENRY IV, AU JUS

BROILED TOP CHOICE CENTER CUT FILET MIGNON
BEARNAISE SAUCE

BREAST OF YOUNG CAPONETTE, CORDON BLEU

BROILED AUSTRALIAN LOBSTER TAILS, DRAWN BUTTER

Idaho Baked Potato or Creole Rice
Primavera Tomato

Desserts

RAINBOW SHERBET

VANILLA ICE CREAM

SAHARA PARFAIT

FAMOUS SWISS CHEESE CAKE

STRAWBERRY SHORT CAKE

CAFE

Roanoke, Virginia 4/11/72: 'As Presley was singing "Release Me", a group of female fans rushed the stage. One of Presley's band members greeted them and nearly wound up in the audience. He was pulled almost off the stage but an acrobatic twist got him back. While this was happening another group charged the other side of the stage toward Presley. Police and members of the show stopped them. Presley stepped toward the rear of the stage, still singing. Police cleared the stage and remained there until the show ended.'

The Sahara Tahoe had contracts with Johnny Carson and Buddy Hackett assuring them the highest pay; others could make as much but not more. After Elvis' negotiations, the Sahara had to raise fees for Hackett and Carson – by $90,000 per week.

Holiday Airlines Schedule

Monday	Lv. L.A.	8:45 A.M.	Arr. Tahoe	11:00 A.M.
		4:00 P.M.		5:40 P.M.
Tuesday	Lv. L.A.	8:45 A.M.	Arr. Tahoe	11:00 A.M.
Wednesday	Lv. L.A.	8:45 A.M.	Arr. Tahoe	11:00 A.M.
Thursday	Lv. L.A.	8:45 A.M.	Arr. Tahoe	11:00 A.M.
		7:00 P.M.		8:40 P.M.
Friday	Lv. L.A.	9:00 A.M.	Arr. Tahoe	10:20 A.M.
		7:45 P.M.		9:05 P.M.
Saturday	Lv. L.A.	8:45 A.M.	Arr. Tahoe	11:00 A.M.
Sunday	Lv. L.A.	9:00 A.M.	Arr. Tahoe	10:20 A.M.
		4:00 P.M.		5:20 P.M.
Monday	Lv. Tahoe	11:30 A.M.	Arr. L.A.	1:10 P.M.
		6:00 P.M.		8:15 P.M.
Tuesday	Lv. Tahoe	6:00 P.M.	Arr. L.A.	8:15 P.M.
Wednesday	Lv. Tahoe	6:00 P.M.	Arr. L.A.	8:15 P.M.
Thursday	Lv. Tahoe	11:30 A.M.	Arr. L.A.	1:10 P.M.
		9:00 P.M.		11:15 P.M.
Friday	Lv. Tahoe	5:45 P.M.	Arr. L.A.	7:25 P.M.
		9:30 P.M.		10:50 P.M.
Saturday	Lv. Tahoe	6:00 P.M.	Arr. L.A.	8:15 P.M.
Sunday	Lv. Tahoe	2:00 P.M.	Arr. L.A.	3:40 P.M.
		8:00 P.M.		9:20 P.M.

TENTATIVE SONG LINEUP - NOVEMBER, 1971 TOUR

1. THAT'S ALLRIGHT MAMA
2. I GOT A WOMAN
3. PROUD MARY
4. LOVE ME TENDER
5. YOU DON'T HAVE TO SAY YOU LOVE ME
6. LOVIN' FEELIN'
7. POLK SALAD ANNIE

    MEDLEY:

        LOVE ME

        HEARTBREAK HOTEL

        JAILHOUSE ROCK

        ONE NIGHT

        HOUND DOG

        HOW GREAT THOU ART

    INTRODUCTIONS

8. JOHNNY B. GOOD
9. IT'S ONLY LOVE
10. SUSPICIOUS MINDS
11. LAWDY MISS CLAWDY
12. BRIDGE OVER TROUBLED WATER
13. CAN'T HELP FALLING IN LOVE

ALTERNATES:

1. I CAN'T STOP LOVING YOU
2. RELEASE ME

ALTERNATES - Continued

3. ARE YOU LONESOME TONIGHT
4. JUST CAN'T HELP BELIEVIN'
5. IMPOSSIBLE DREAM
6. IT'S NOW OR NEVER
7. LITTLE SISTER
8. I'M LEAVIN'
9. I, JOHN
10. FOR THE FIRST TIME
11. SWEET CAROLINE
12. SOMETHIN'

OPENING TONIGHT

DEL WEBB'S SAHARA TAHOE

ELVIS

NOW RESERVATIONS NOW

GOOD GUY/50 from 91 KISN

HERE COMES THE KING

NOVEMBER 11th, MEMORIAL COLISEUM

OREGON

Western Union Telegram

SI8293 1109P EDJUN 10 72 NYD366(1946)(1-011062D162-050)PD 06/10/72 198
ICS IPMNYNE NYK

RETRIEVAL REPLY
PARTIAL DELIVERY
1-009514A162 NYG 362 ICS IPMTBZU
ZCZC 03037 B 2124997151 PD TDMT BROOKLYN NY 10 1230P EDT
PMS ELVIS PRESLEY MADISON SQUARE GARDEN, DLR
NYK

SAW YOU LIVE FOR FIRST TIME LAST NIGHT. LOVED YOU EVEN MORE. COME
BACK SOON. CONGRATULATIONS AND GOD BLESS
MARIE RYAN.

ELVIS PRESLEY SHOW

Sahara Tahoe - Stateline, Nev.

July, 1971

THE FOLLOWING ARE TO BE CLEARED FOR ALL REHEARSALS OF THE ELVIS
PRESLEY SHOW AS PER SCHEDULE. HOWEVER, THEY ARE NOT AUTHORIZED
TO BRING VISITORS, NOR ARE VISITORS ALLOWED AT THESE REHEARSAL
SESSIONS.

MUSICIANS: JAMES BURTON   JOE ESPOSITO
          JERRY SCHEFF   SONNY WEST
          RONNIE TUTT   LAMAR FIKE
          GLEN HARDIN   JERRY SCHILLING
          JOHN WILKINSON   RED WEST
          CHARLEY HODGE   HAMBURGER JAMES
          JOE GUERCIO   GEE GEE GAMBOL
          JOE OSBORNE
                                 COLONEL PARKER
SINGERS: MYRNA SMITH   TOM DISKIN
          SYLVIA SHEMWELL   GEORGE BARKHILL
          ESTELLE BROWN   JIM O'BRIEN
          ANN WILLIAMS   BILL MC PHERSON

          JOE MOSCHEO
          ARMAND MORALES
          GREG GORDON
          JIM MURRAY
          TERRY BLACKWOOD

          KATHY WESTMORELAND

OTHERS: AL PACHUCKI
          BILL PORTER
          HOTEL SOUND MAN

IN THE SHOW ROOM MEMBERS OF THE HOUSE BAND WILL BE IDENTIFIED BY
JOE GUERCIO WHERE NECESSARY.

NO OTHER VISITORS PLEASE

8-9-71

1 That's alright
2 Proud Mary
3 Jailhouse Rock
4 Love me tender
5 You don't have to say you love me
6 Lost that lovin' feelin'
7 Polk Salad Annie
8 Johnny Be Goode
9

medley   Love me
                Blue Suede Shoes
                Heartbreak Hotel
                Teddy Bear
                Don't be cruel
                One night
                Hound Dog
10 Suspicious mind
10. It's over
12 Family ... — Jim Lewis
13 Can't Stop loving you
14 Bridge over ...

Aug. 5, th   LasVegas

1. THAT's ALRIGHT MAMA   2:20
2. MYSTERY TRAIN - TIGERMAN   2:20
3. The WONDER OF YOU (11:50)   1:35
4. THE NEXT STEP is LOVE   3:20
5. LOVE ME TENDER   2:15

6. WORD's   2:30
7. LOST THAT lovin FEELIN (12:15) 4:00
8. YOU don't HAVE to SAY YOU LOVE ME 2:00
9. POLK SALAD ANNE   3:45
        (INTRO's)
10. I'VE LOST YOU   3:30
11 BRIDGE over TROUBLED WATER's 4:15
12 PATCH iT uP   (14:00)   4:15
13 CAN't HELP FALLING IN LOVE

Milestone Dates: June 1972 - Madison Square Garden

The Sweet Inspirations conquered Madison Square Garden, including the specially added 2078 extra seats. But when they finished, the audience's desire for Elvis was piqued, and they chased comedian Jackie Kahane from the stage. Interrupted by claps and catcalls, he said, 'All right, friends, I'm going to be here a few minutes...' but they responded, 'We want Elvis.' Kahane said, 'You are 20,000. I am one. That's pretty rough odds.' And he left.

Elvis – unannounced, unrivalled – appeared in a white suit with gold studs, a deep V front, a gold scarf, a white cape lined in gold, a wide gold belt and white boots. He was a Vegas-ized Memphis, his rough rock and roll roots covered by panache.

Whether playing to hundreds or tens of thousands, Elvis reached each fan individually. He created intimacy on his overflowing stage. To play a solo acoustic number, Charlie Hodge had to reach around Elvis, hand-holding a microphone to the strings. Elvis can't have his own mike stand?

He premiered at Madison Square Garden for four shows, June 9th through 11th, reaching more than 80,000 people. Tickets went on sale May 9th, and 2000 people mobbed the box office before dawn.

But the intimacy lets the audience feel the bond between two old friends. Hodge looks at Elvis, laughing louder than anyone. See us old pranksters? We can't believe we're up here either.

The night after he finished at the 'Garden, Elvis appeared in Fort Wayne, Indiana, 7690 in the audience, not even a sell-out. Here, ten dollars was costly and reviewers found Jackie Kahane funny. Elvis' lack of discrimination in songs reflected the diverse audiences he played to.

Variety: 'He would strike those unforgettable Elvis poses. Right leg forward, left leg thrown back shaking to the music and – the flashbulbs went off and the shrieks getting higher and the scene more intense – one was struck with the thought that possibly here was a guy who, if he was so inclined, could have made the place fall down... He stood there at the end, his arms stretched out, the great gold cloak giving him wings, a champion, the only one in his class.'

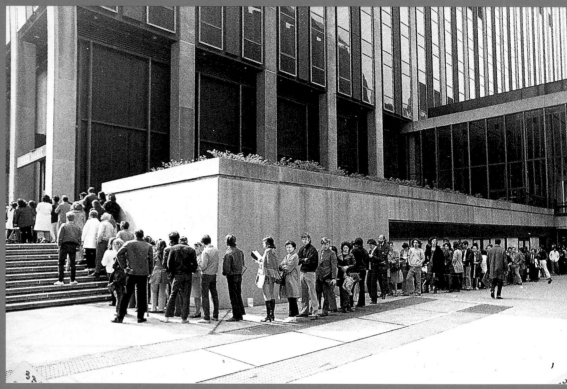

Standing in line round the block at the 'Garden

The *New York Times* ran a whole page review

The shows were the only live concerts Elvis ever performed in New York City

'In a white cape and jumpsuit, (he was) covered throughout the concert by a blinding fusilade of strobe lights'

With *Aloha From Hawaii*, the kid from Memphis was steering a satellite. Television brought Elvis to his fans in the 1950s, had announced his return in 1968, and in 1973, it proved him a cultural icon as grand as any other in the world. Employing satellite technology that had been previously reserved for political and financial use, *Aloha* beamed Elvis to an estimated billion and a half fans, screaming, shouting, and dancing in the comfort of their own homes.

Honolulu was chosen as the site, ostensibly, because the time zone made it convenient for reaching Asia, Africa, and Australia, and because the satellite signal could be easily transmitted over the North Pole. But a deeper reasoning is revealed through the pictures of Elvis with a lei around his neck, with the natives in grass skirts, with the lovely Pacific Ocean as a backdrop: Success. Leisure. Dreamy contentment. America is a country without castles and ancient ruins, and no other locale within its borders could convey the natural magesty appropriate for the King.

To announce the event, Elvis and the Colonel held two press conferences, first at the Hilton Hawaiian Village, (the day after closing his 1972 fall tour with three sold-out shows in Honolulu) then in Las Vegas. 'Folks, get a seat and sit down,' said Colonel at the Hilton, 'or you'll have to pay five dollars for standing up.' Appearing with Elvis was RCA Records chief Rocco Laginestra, who announced that among countries negotiating a transmission were China and the USSR.

Longtime Hawaiian journalist Eddie Sherman remembered when Elvis had raised over $62,000 for the Pearl Harbor memorial. He informed Colonel Parker of a Hawaiian hospital's cancer research fund that had been established in the name of a recent victim, the Hawaiian singer and songwriter Kui Lee; for some time Elvis had been performing Lee's 'I'll Remember You.' Two days later, Sherman was called to a meeting; 'I was stunned at the news they gave me,' he wrote in

The Honolulu International Center Arena fills up

Elvis greets RCA president Rocco Laginestra

The Las Vegas press conference

Thirteen signs in seven languages flashed 'Elvis.' The foreign spellings alone used over 2,200 colored bulbs.

The backdrop included a twenty-foot dancing, guitar playing silhouette of the star sculpted from lights

No expense was spared. There was even a specially designed ticket-stub that became instantly collectable.

his column. 'They decided to turn over ALL proceeds of the show (including programs, pictures, etc.) to the 'Kui Lee Cancer Fund.' The takings of the warm-up rehearsal show were also contributed to the fund.

There were no free tickets. Elvis and the Colonel kicked off with a $1,000 donation, and RCA matched it. Two thousand plants in five gallon cans were spread throughout the auditorium. A runway was built so Elvis could better interact with his audience. Though it was recorded in January, the American broadcast was withheld until the April ratings sweeps.

There's a brief moment after 'C. C. Rider' when you think Elvis is going to smash his black acoustic guitar. But he's not a punk rock band. It's a flash of his youthful energy, of the nation's youthful energy, of yesterday, but also of now. Aloha's album art (using an existing picture, not one from the show, to speed up the release) says it all: Elvis, bouncing off the world and into outer space, King of the Universe.

'One lady with five kids only had $3.75, but wanted five tickets... she got 'em. Another youngster had only 80 cents to donate. He got a ticket. One girl with only $1.19 asked for two tickets. Granted.'

The *Aloha* broadcast was, in its way, as historic a TV event as the '68 Comeback

DEPARTMENT OF AUDITORIUMS
CITY AND COUNTY OF HONOLULU
777 WARD AVENUE
HONOLULU, HAWAII 96814

FRANK F. FASI
MAYOR

RICHARD K. SHARPLESS
MANAGING DIRECTOR

MATTHEW ESPORITO
DIRECTOR

January 11, 1973

Elvis and The Colonel
RCA Record Tours
Mr. George Parkhill
Hilton Hawaiian Village
Honolulu, Hawaii

Gentlemen,

For your information I take great pleasure to advise all of you, That the donations for both the Satellite Telecast and the Dress Rehearsal will exceed $75,000.00 which I think is wonderful. 100% of these donations will be turned over to the Kui Lee Cancer Fund.

Very Truly Yours,

Arthur W. Samuel
Box Office Manager
Honolulu International Center

RCA Records | 1133 Avenue of The Americas | New York, NY 10036 | Telephone (212) 586-3000

GEORGE L. PARKHILL
Director
RCA Record Tours
and
Artist Relations

RCA

HONOLULU, HAWAII
NOVEMBER 20, 1972

ALOHA!!!

FOR YOUR INFORMATION.....

JANUARY 14, 1973, AT 12:30 AM, HONOLULU, HAWAII, ELVIS' WORLDWIDE SATELLITE CONCERT WILL BE PRESENTED LIVE BY RCA RECORD TOURS FROM THE HONOLULU INTERNATIONAL CENTER.

AUDIENCE ATTENDANCE AT THIS CONCERT WILL BE BY DONATION ONLY. ALL DONATIONS WILL BE USED FOR THE KUI LEE CANCER FUND IN HONOLULU, HAWAII.

THE NEED FOR THESE FUNDS WAS BROUGHT TO THE ATTENTION OF COLONEL PARKER BY EDDIE SHERMAN IN A LETTER WRITTEN SEVERAL MONTHS AGO. RCA RECORD TOURS, ELVIS AND THE COLONEL ARE DELIGHTED TO BE ABLE TO PARTICIPATE IN THIS WORTHY PROJECT, JUST AS THEY DID IN 1961 FOR THE ARIZONA MEMORIAL.

THE GOAL FOR THIS PROJECT IS $25,000. MR. ROCCO LAGINESTRA, PRESIDENT OF RCA RECORDS, AND ELVIS PRESLEY ARE STARTING OFF THIS FUND TODAY WITH A DONATION OF $1,000 EACH.

---

as of 1/11 7 PM

REVISED SCHEDULE -- ELVIS-ALOHA FROM HAWAII-VIA SATELLITE

SATURDAY & SUNDAY, JANUARY 13,14, 1973   H.I.C. ARENA

10:00 AM - 10:30 AM	TRAVEL TO HIC ARENA (TD, AD, 2 VEH, Audio, Maintenance)
10:30 AM - 11:30 AM	CHECKOUT MACHINES FOR EDITING
11:30 AM - 3:00 PM	COMPOSITE EDIT - ELVIS
3:00 PM - 4:00 PM	L U N C H
3:30 PM - 4:00 PM	CREW TRAVEL TO HIC ARENA
4:00 PM - 6:00 PM	ESU & TECH PROD. MEETING
6:00 PM - 8:30 PM	RUNTHRU W/CAMERAS ELVIS SINGERS & MUSICIANS IN FULL WARDROBE
8:30 PM - 9:30 PM	D I N N E R (CATERED)
9:30 PM	GROUPS MEET OUTSIDE (ETHNIC, HULA GIRLS, ROYAL HAWAIIAN BAND)
9:30 PM - 10:00 PM	TP EXTERIOR CAMERA
10:00 PM - 11:00 PM	VTR: EXTERIOR - AUDIENCE IN
11:00 PM - 12:00 M	EDIT EXTERIOR TO OPENING
11:00 PM	ELVIS SINGERS & MUSICIANS TO MAKEUP
11:00 PM - 12:00 M	TP + TURNAROUND EXTERIOR TO INTERIOR
11:30 PM	ELVIS PRESLEY TO MAKEUP & WARDROBE
11:30 PM - 12:15 AM	HARRY BLACKSTONE WARMUP AUDIENCE
12:20 AM - 12:25 AM	WARMUP
12:25 AM - 12:30 AM	SATELLITE FEED (AUDIENCE SHOTS)
12:30 AM - 1:30 AM	VTR: AIR - FEED TO SATELLITE
1:30 AM - 1:40 AM	SATELLITE FEED (AUDIENCE SHOTS)
1:30 AM - 2:00 AM	IA WRAP
2:00 AM - DONE	TECH WRAP
12:00 N - 12:00 M	IA SCENERY-STRIKE

INDIVIDUAL CALLS

6:00 PM	ELVIS SINGERS & MUSICIANS	12:15 AM ORCHESTRA (IN WARDROBE)
9:30 PM	GROUPS MEET OUTSIDE	
11:00 PM	ELVIS SINGERS & MUSICIANS (2ND CALL FOR MAKEUP)	
11:30 PM	ELVIS (MAKEUP & WARDROBE)	

MAHALO
HAWAII
Thank You   *Thank You*

FOR DONATING MORE THAN

$75,000*

THE ORIGINAL GOAL WAS $25,000

To The KUI LEE Cancer Fund

Without all the people in Hawaii
it would not have been possible!

WE ARE PROUD TO BE OF HELP
ELVIS and the COLONEL
RCA RECORD TOURS and all our associates

*100% to the Kui Lee Cancer Fund
No Deductions For Any Expenses

Thank You   Thank You

Mahalo

Elvis and the colonel

OFFICE OF THE MAYOR
City and County of Honolulu

P R O C L A M A T I O N

WHEREAS, Elvis Presley has helped spread the beauty and aloha of Hawaii throughout the world through his films and recordings; and

WHEREAS, in addition to being one of the world's greatest entertainers he has also been among its most benevolent humanitarians; and

WHEREAS, he has often proven his affection for the people of Honolulu, including his role in the construction of the U.S.S. Arizona Memorial; and

WHEREAS, he is scheduled to perform before an estimated 1.5 billion people in an international telecast, January 14, emanating from the Honolulu International Center in Honolulu,

NOW, THEREFORE, I, FRANK F. FASI, Mayor of the City and County of Honolulu, hereby proclaim January 13, 1973, as

ELVIS PRESLEY DAY

in the City and County of Honolulu and offer sincere appreciation that he has graciously donated all proceeds from his show to the Kui Lee Memorial Cancer Fund. I further call upon all the people of Honolulu to strongly support Hawaii's great adopted son and the charity he has so generously assisted.

IN WITNESS WHEREOF, I have hereunto set my hand and caused the seal of the City and County of Honolulu to be affixed.

Done this 12th day of January, 1973, in Honolulu, Hawaii.

FRANK F. FASI, Mayor
City and County of Honolulu

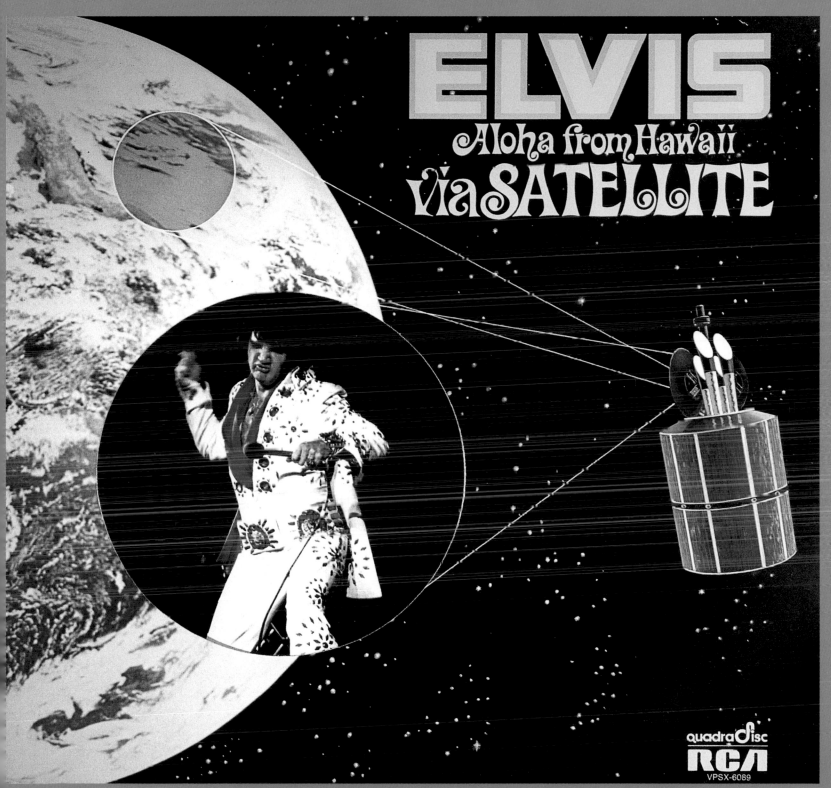

Colonel recorded the concert, hoping to release in six days. With three pressing plants on overtime, it still took a week and a half

'Laced in radiant costume, webbed in lights

... immersed in waves of sound...

he four year old Lisa Marie first saw Elvis perform on November 15th, 1972, his second night in Long Beach, California. From stage, he announced it was 'the first time she's seen her daddy make a fool of himself in front of 15,000 people.' Ironically, his marriage to Priscilla was at an end with an impending divorce.

Elvis returned to Tahoe in 1973 (May 4-20). Billboards organised by Colonel flashed Elvis' name all over the desert in twenty-four foot letters, red, so that no one could fail to know he was performing. (Soon, even his Las Vegas ads were being printed in psychedelic glow-in-the-dark ink.) The Sahara Tahoe had 300,000 phone calls about Elvis's gigs – it seated 61,000.

The madness continued. In Nashville, the local promoter returned $300,000 of overflow money when his two shows sold out. 'Never!' he said. 'Never again will I get into anything like this.'

Every day was Elvis day. Jimmy Carter, then

...and the Las Vegas Hilton
the International Hotel
cordially invite you and a guest
to Elvis' opening show
January 26, 1972
•
Cocktails at your table 7:30 pm
Dinner at 8:30 pm
R.S.V.P.
Envelope Enclosed

'... he will assault the senses into insensibility
with an unforgettable display'

Special Photo Folio Pocket Edition

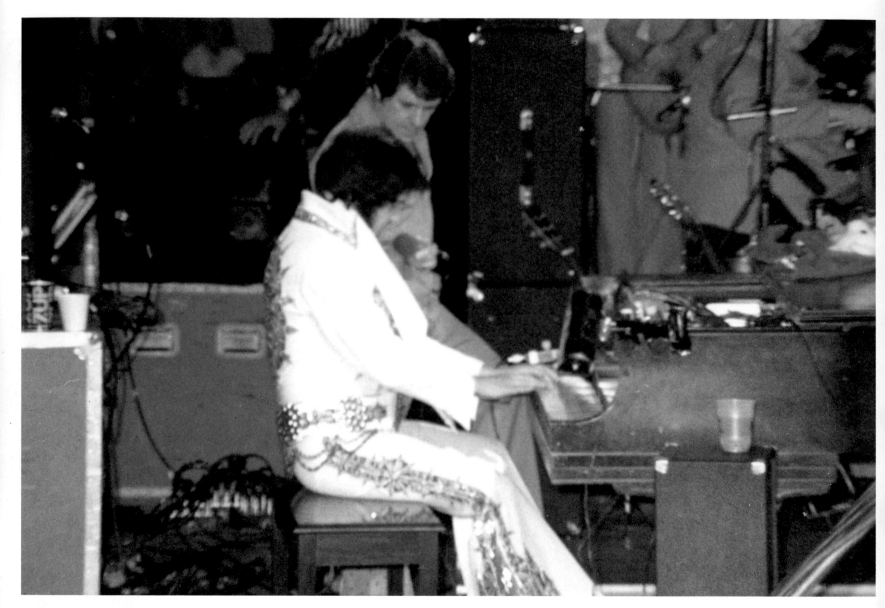

Elvis flew between shows, his entourage requiring three jets: one for Colonel Parker and his staff, one for the supporting acts, one for Elvis and whomever he selected to join him.

1970-77 Superstar

Governor of Georgia, made January 8, 1974 Elvis Presley Day. North Carolina declared March 9-15, 1974 Elvis Week. In October 1973, Elvis was admitted to a Memphis hospital for recurrent pneumonia, a condition not helped by increasing drug use.

In Roanoke, his plan to dine out was scrapped when the hotel was surrounded by fans. A taxi was dispatched, returning with fifty hamburgers and the local supply of bottled mineral water for star and entourage. In Murfreesboro, about thirty miles outside of Nashville, 25,000 came to his two shows, roughly equalling the town's population.

Finally, on March 16, 1974, Elvis played Memphis, five shows over three days. He hadn't played his hometown in thirteen years, since his 1961 charity shows. He may have gained weight, become physically unfit, but he was always a symbol of sex, of youth, of energy, of honesty. When he greeted his audience, his remarks were simple: 'It's a pleasure to be at home again for the first time in a long time.' He tried to talk again

from the stage, but audience enthusiasm prevented him. Through a local journalist, he was able to convey a message. 'I wanted to record a live session in my hometown of Memphis… this is where it all started out for me.'

When he returned to L.A. for some May dates, Led Zeppelin's Robert Plant and Jimmy Page sat on the ninth row. Paul Rodgers of Bad Company was also there. Elvis's closing song was the Rick Nelson hit, 'Fools Rush In.'

Darkening Road

January 1975, Elvis was again admitted to a Memphis hospital. He was known to be in pain and rumours circulated that it was his liver, that he had leukemia or hepatitis. Doctors discovered that his lower colon was twisted. Several days later, Vernon had a heart attack. Elvis tended toward darker jumpsuits. He was more and more sickly, and working the road harder and harder. He was forty years old. At a show in Memphis, he bent down to kiss a fan and split his pants.

Double duty on weekends was still the norm. His thoughts never left others, and on May 5, 1975, he raised $110,000 for tornado victims in Mississippi.

On June 26, 1977, Elvis finished a ten-day/ten-city tour in Indianapolis. Since April of the previous year, he'd been doing roughly two weeks on, two weeks off. A hunk of burning energy, Elvis Presley touched all people. His audience spanned generations and races, finding in him something that nothing else in an increasingly stratified society offered. What had been remarkable in 1956 was remarkable a lifetime later, and if it couldn't have happened without the man on stage, nor could it have happened without the people in the audience. Every individual in the thousands and thousands who saw him, in the hundreds whom he employed, himself being at the top of the list – a need was satisfied. The mayhem that surrounded him did not conceal the peace that he brought from town to town, from arena to arena, from fan to fan.

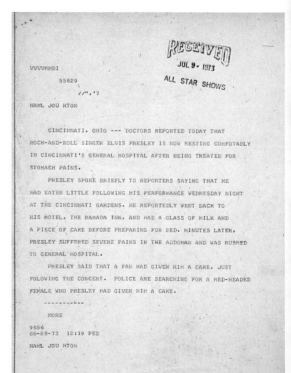

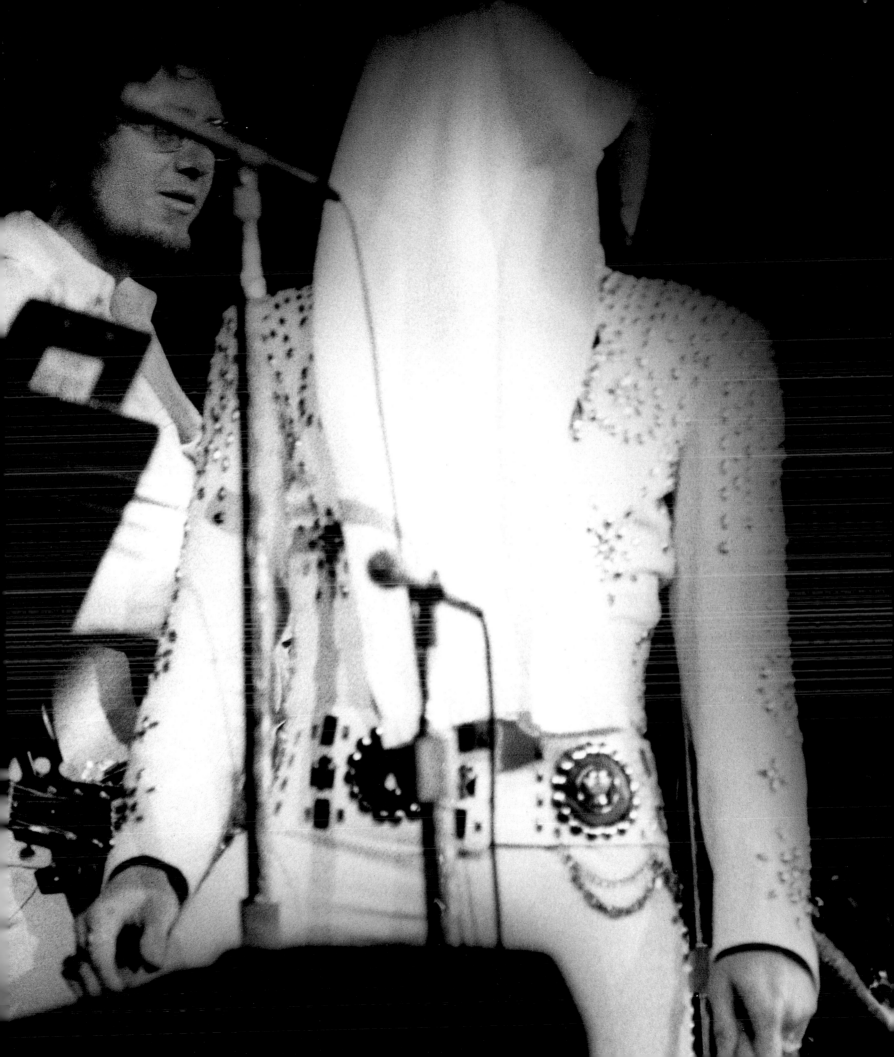

After an unusual two months off in the summer of 1977, Elvis was gearing up for his next two week stint, to begin August 17 with a couple of gigs in the Pacific Northwest, followed by an appearance the next night in New York state, winding up ten days later with another Memphis homecoming. Since 1970, he had performed a total of 1094 shows in no less than 130 cities.

But Elvis was called home before he could alight. On August 16th, the superhero spread his cape one last time, encompassing in his dreams the dreams of all his fans, making his message their message, giving voice to those who feared to speak. It is a testament to this one human being's power that his following has not diminished in the years since his death. Not diminished and, in plain fact, strengthened. Elvis has left the planet, but like the promise in the clothesline's rainbow, Elvis lives, Elvis lives, the king lives on.

Concert Log

Showdates 1954

07-17	MEMPHIS, TN–Bon Air
07-24	MEMPHIS, TN–Bon Air
07-30	MEMPHIS, TN-Overton Park
07-31	MEMPHIS, TN–Bon Air
08-07	MEMPHIS, TN-Eagles Nest
08-27	MEMPHIS, TN-Eagles Nest
09-09	MEMPHIS, TN-Katz Drug Store
09-10	MEMPHIS, TN-Eagles Nest
09-11	MEMPHIS, TN-Eagles Nest
09-18	MEMPHIS, TN-Eagles Nest
09-24	MEMPHIS, TN-Eagles Nest
09-25	MEMPHIS, TN-Eagles Nest
10-01	MEMPHIS, TN-Eagles Nest
10-02	NASHVILLE, TN-Grand Ole Opry
10-06	MEMPHIS, TN-Eagles Nest
10-09	MEMPHIS, TN-Eagles Nest
10-13	MEMPHIS, TN-Eagles Nest
10-15	MEMPHIS, TN-Eagles Nest
10-16	SHREVEPORT, LA-The Louisiana Hayride
10-29	MEMPHIS, TN-Eagles Nest
10-30	MEMPHIS, TN-Eagles Nest
11-06	SHREVEPORT, LA-The Louisiana Hayride
11-08	MEMPHIS, TN-Memphis State-Bloodbank
11-12?	GLADEWATER, TX-The Mint Club
11-13	SHREVEPORT, LA-The Louisiana Hayride
11-17	MEMPHIS, TN-Eagles Nest
11-19	LAKE CLIFF (near Shreveport), LA - Club
11-20	SHREVEPORT, LA-The Louisiana Hayride
11-24	TEXARKANA, AR-
11-25	HOUSTON, TX-The Paladium
11-26	HOUSTON, TX-The Paladium
11-27	HOUSTON, TX-The Paladium
12-02	HELENA, AR-Catholic Club
12-04	SHREVEPORT, LA-The Louisiana Hayride
12-10	MEMPHIS, TN-Eagles Nest
12-11	SHREVEPORT, LA-The Louisiana Hayride
12-18	SHREVEPORT, LA-The Louisiana Hayride
12-28	HOUSTON, TX-Cooks Hoedown

Showdates 1955

01-01	HOUSTON, TX-Eagles Hall
01-05	SAN ANGELO, TX-City Auditorium
01-06	LUBBOCK, TX-Fair Park Auditorium
01-07	MIDLAND, TX-Midland High School Auditorium
01-08	SHREVEPORT, LA-The Louisiana Hayride
01-12	CLARKSDALE, MS-Clarksdale Auditorium
01-13	HELENA, AR-Catholic Club

01-15	SHREVEPORT, LA-The Louisiana Hayride
01-17	BOONEVILLE, MS-Junior College
01-18	CORINTH, MS- Alcorn County Courthouse
01-19	SHEFFIELD, AL-Sheffield Community Center
01-20	LEACHVILLE, AL-High School Gymnasium
01-21	SIKESTON, MO-The Armory
01-22	SHREVEPORT, LA-The Louisiana Hayride
01-24	HAWKINS, TX-Humble Camp Recreation Hall
01-25	TYLER, TX -Mayfair Building
01-26	GILMER, TX -REA Building
01-27	LONGVIEW, TX -Reo Palm Isle Club
01-28	GASTON, TX -Hi School
01-29	SHREVEPORT, LA -The Louisiana Hayride
02-01	RANDOLPH, MS -Hi School
02-02	AUGUSTA, AR-Augusta High School
02-04	NEW ORLEANS, LA
02-05	SHREVEPORT, LA-The Louisiana Hayride
02-06	MEMPHIS, TN-North Hall Auditorium
02-07	RIPLEY, MS-Ripley Gymnasium
02-10	ALPINE, TX-High School Auditorium
02-11	CARLSBAD, NM- Sports Arena
02-11	HOBBS, NM -
02-12	CARLSBAD, NM-Legion's Hut
02-13	LUBBOCK, TX-Fair Park Coliseum
02-14	ROSWELL, NM-North Junior
	Highschool Auditorium
02-15	ABILENE, TX-Fairpark Auditorium
02-16	ODESSA, TX-Odessa Senior High School, Field House
02-17	SAN ANGELO, TX-City Auditorium
02-18	MONROE, LA-West Monroe Highschool
	Auditorium
02-19	SHREVEPORT, LA-The Louisiana Hayride
02-20	LITTLE ROCK, AR-Robinson Auditorium
02-21	CAMDEN, AR-City Auditorium
02-22	HOPE, AR-Hope City Hall
02-23	PINEBLUFF, AR-Pine Bluff High School Auditorium
02-24	BASTROP, LA-Southside Elementary School
02-26	CLEVELAND, OH-Cirle Theater Jamboree
03-02	NEWPORT, AR-U.S.Armory and Porgies Rooftop
03-04	DE KALB, TX-High School Auditorium
03-05	SHREVEPORT, LA-The Louisiana Hayride
03-07	PARIS, TN-Paris City Auditorium
03-08	HELENA, AR-Catholic Club
03-09	POPLAR BLUFF, MO-The Armory
03-10	CLARKSDALE, MS-City Auditorium
03-11	ALEXANDRIA, LA-Jimmie Thompson's Arena
03-12	SHREVEPORT, LA-The Louisiana Hayride
03-17	AUSTIN, TX - Dessau Hall

03-19	HOUSTON, TX-Eagles Hall
03-21	PARKIN, AR–High School Auditorium
03-28	BIG CREEK, MS-High School Gymnasium
03-29	TOCOPOLA, MS-High School Gymnasium
03-30	ELDORADO, AR-High School Auditorium
03-31	LONGVIEW, TX - Reo Palm Isle
04-01	ODESSA, TX-Piece Ector County Auditorium
04-02	HOUSTON, TX-The Louisiana Hayride
	(remote broadcast)
04-07	CORINTH, MS-Alcorn County Courthouse
04-08	GOBLER, MO- B'n'B Club
04-09	SHREVEPORT, LA-The Louisiana Hayride
04-13	BRECKENRIDGE, TX-High School Auditorium
04-14	GAINESVILLE, TX-Owl Park
04-15	STAMFORD, TX-High School Auditorium
	and The Round Up Hall
04-16	DALLAS, TX-The Big D Jamboree (8:00)
	Round Up Club (10:30)
04-20	GRENADA, MS-American Legion Hut
04-23	WACO, TX- Heart O' Texas Coliseum (Hayride remote)
04-24	HOUSTON, TX- Cooks Hoedown and Magnolia Gardens
04-25	WICHITA FALLS, TX-M.B. Corral
04-25	SEYMOUR, TX - High School Auditorium
04-26	BIG SPRINGS, TX-City Auditorium
04-29	LUBBOCK, TX-The Cotton Club
04-30	GLADEWATER, TX-The Louisiana Hayrire
	(remote broadcast)
05-01	NEW ORLEANS, LA-Municipal Auditorium
05-02	BATON ROUGE, LA-Baton Rouge High
	School Auditorium
05-04	MOBILE, AL-Ladd Stadium
05-05	MOBILE, AL-Ladd Stadium
05-07	DAYTONA BEACH, FL-The Peabody Auditorium
05-08	TAMPA, FL-Ft. Homer Hesterly Armory
05-09	FORT MYERS, FL-New City Auditorium
05-10	OCALA, FL-Southeastern Pavillion
05-11	ORLANDO, FL-City Auditorium
05-12	JACKSONVILLE, FL-New Ball Park
05-13	JACKSONVILLE, FL-New Ball Park
05-14	NEW BERN, NC-Shrine Auditorium
05-15	NORFOLK, VA-Norfolk Auditorium
05-16	RICHMOND, VA-The Mosque Theater
05-17	ASHEVILLE, NC-City Auditorium
05-18	ROANOKE, VA-American Legion Auditorium
05-19	RALEIGH, NC-Memorial Auditorium
05-21	SHREVEPORT, LA-The Louisiana Hayride
05-22	HOUSTON, TX-Magnolia Gardens
05-26	MERIDIAN, MI-Jimmie Rodgers Memorial Celebration

05-29	FORT WORTH, TX-North Side Col. 4.PM
	DALLAS, TX-The Sportatorium. 8.PM
05-30	ABILENE, TX-Fair Park Auditorium
05-31	MIDLAND, TX-Midland Highschool Auditorium 7.30PM
	ODESSA, TX-High School Field House. 8.30PM
06-01	GUYMON, OK-High School Auditorium
06-02	AMARILLO, TX-City Auditorium
06-03	LUBBOCK, TX-JOHNSON-CONNELLEY
	Pontiac Show Room 7P.M.
	LUBBOCK, TX, Fairpark Col. 8.PM
06-04	SHREVEPORT, LA-The Louisiana Hayride
06-05	HOPE, AR-The Coliseum
06-08	SWEETWATER, TX-Auditorium
06-10	BRECKENRIDGE, TX- American Legion Hall
06-11	SHREVEPORT, LA-The Louisiana Hayride
06-14	BRUCE, MS-Highschool Gymnasium
06-15	BELDEN, MS-High School Gymnasium
06-17	STAMFORD, TX-Roundup Hall
06-18	DALLAS, TX-The Big D Jamboree
06-19	HOUSTON, TX-Magnolia Gardens
06-20	BEAUMONT, TX-City Auditorium
06-21	BEAUMONT, TX-City Auditorium
06-23	LAWTON, OK- McMahon Auditorium
	and The Southern Club
06-24	ALTUS,-OK
06-25	SHREVEPORT, LA-The Louisiana Hayride
06-26	BILOXI, MI-SLAVONIAN LODGE
06-27	KEESLER, MI-Air Force Base
06-28	KEESLER, MI-Air Force Base
06-29	MOBILE, AL-Curtis Gordon's Radio Ranch
06-30	MOBILE, AL-Curtis Gordon's Radio Ranch
07-01	PLAQUEMINE, LA - Casino Club
07-02	SHREVEPORT, LA-The Louisiana Hayride
07-03	CORPUS CHRISTI, TX-Hoedown Club
07-04	DE LEON, TX-Hodges Park
	STEPHENVILLE, TX-City Recreational Building
	BROWNWOOD, TX-Memorial Hall - 8.PM
07-20	CAPE GIRARDEAU, MO-Cape Arena Building
07-21	NEWPORT, AR-Silver Moon Club
07-23	DALLAS, TX-The Big Jamboree
07-25	FORT MYERS, FL-New City Auditorium
07-26	ORLANDO, FL-Municipal Auditorium
07-27	ORLANDO, FL-Municipal Auditorium
07-28	JACKSONVILLE, FL-New Baseball Stadium
07-29	JACKSONVILLE, FL-New Baseball Stadium
07-30	DAYTONA BEACH, FL-Peabody Auditorium
07-31	TAMPA, FL- Ft. Hesterly Armory
08-01	TUPELO, MS-Mississippi-Alabama Fairgrounds
08-02	SHEFFIELD, AL-Sheffield Community Center
08-03	LITTLE ROCK, AR-Robinson Auditorium
08-04	CAMDEN, AR-Municipal Auditorium
08-05	MEMPHIS, TN-Overton Park Shell
08-06	BATESVILLE, AR-River Stadium
08-07	HOUSTON, TX-Magnolia Gardens
	HOUSTON, TX-Cooks Hoedown Club
08-08	TYLER, TX-Mayfair Building
08-09	HENDERSON, TX - Rodeo Arena
08-10	GLADEWATER, TX-Baseball Park
08-11	LONGVIEW, TX - Reo Palm Isle
08-12	KILGORE, TX - Driller Park
08-20	SHREVEPORT, LA-The Louisiana Hayride
08-22	WICHITA FALLS, TX-Spudder Park
08-23	BRYAN, TX
08-24	CONROE, TX-Davy Crockett Hi School F.B. Stadium
08-25	AUSTIN, TX-The Sportscenter
08-26	GONZALES, TX-Baseball Park
08-27	SHREVEPORT, LA Hayride
09-01	NEW ORLEANS, LA-Porchartrain Beach
09-02	TEXARKANA, AR-Municipal Auditorium
09-03	DALLAS, TX- The Big Jamboree
	DALLAS, TX- The Round Up Club
09-05	FORREST CITY, AR-Smith Stadium at F.C. High School
09-06	BONO, AR-High School Gymnasium
09-07	SIKESTON, MO-The Armory
09-08	CLARKSDALE, MI-City Auditorium
09-09	MC COMB, MI-High School Auditorium
09-10	SHREVEPORT, LA-The Louisiana Hayride
09-11	NORFOLK, VA-Norfolk Auditorium
09-12	NORFOLK, VA-Norfolk Auditorium
09-13	NEW BERN, NC-Shrine Auditorium
09-14	WILSON, NC-Fleming Stadium
09-15	ROANOKE, VA-American Legion Auditorium
09-16	ASHEVILLE, NC-City Auditorium
09-17	THOMASVILLE, NC
09-18	RICHMOND, VA-WRVA Auditorium
09-19	RICHMOND, VA-WRVA Auditorium
09-20	DANVILLE, VA-WDVS Barn, Danville Fairgrounds
09-21	RALEIGH, Memorial Auditorium
09-22	KINGSPORT, TN-Civic Auditorium
09-24	SHREVEPORT, LA-The Louisiana Hayride
09-26	GILMER, TX-Junior High Gymnasium
09-28	GOBLER, MO- B & B Club
10-01	SHREVEPORT, LA-Hayride
10-03	BRYAN, TX-White Coliseum
10-04	PARIS, TX-Boys Club Gymnasium
10-05	GREENVILLE, TX-City Auditorium
10-06	AUSTIN, TX-San Marcos College and Skyline Club
10-08	HOUSTON, TX. - City Auditorium – Hayride Remote
10-10	BROWNWOOD, TX-Memorial Hall
10-11	ABILENE, TX-Fair Park Auditorium
10-12	MIDLAND, TX-High School Auditorium
10-13	AMARILLO, TX-City Auditorium
10-14	ODESSA, TX-High School Fieldhouse
10-15	LUBBOCK, TX-Fair Park Auditorium
10-16	OKLAHOMA CITY, OK-Municipal Auditorium
10-17	EL DORADO, AR-Memorial Stadium
10-19	CLEVELAND, OH-Circle Theater
10-20	CLEVELAND, OH-Brooklyn High and St. Michaels Hall
10-21	ST. LOUIS, MO-Missouri Theater
10-22	ST. LOUIS, MO-Missouri Theater
10-23	ST. LOUIS, MO-Missouri Theater
10-24	NEWPORT, AR-Silver Moon Club
10-26	PRICHARD, AL-Greater Gulf States Fair
10-27	JACKSON, AL-
10-29	SHREVEPORT, LA-The Louisiana Hayride
11-05	SHREVEPORT, LA-The Louisiana Hayride
11-06	BILOXI, MI-Biloxi Community House
11-07	KEESLER, MI-Air Force Base
11-08	KEESLER, MI-Air Force Base
11-12	CARTHAGE ,TX-Afternoon show Opening Of Milling Co.
	SHREVEPORT, LA The Louisiana Hayride
11-13	MEMPHIS, TN-Ellis Auditorium
11-14	FORREST CITY, AR-F.C. High School Auditorium
11-15	SHEFFIELD, AL-Sheffield Community Center
11-16	CAMDEN, AR-Camden City Auditorium
11-17	TEXARKANA, AR-Arkansas Municipal Auditorium
11-18	LONGVIEW, TX-Reo-Palm Isle
11-19	GLADEWATER, TX-The Louisiana Hayride (Remote)
11-25	PORT ARTHUR, TX-Woodrow Wilson High School
11-26	SHREVEPORT, LA-The Louisiana Hayride
11-29	RICMOND, VA-The Mosque Theater for Philip Morris
12-02	ATLANTA, GA-Atlanta's Sports Arena
12-03	MONTGOMERY, AL-State Coliseum
12-04	INDIANAPOLIS, IN-The Lyric Theater
12-05	INDIANAPOLIS, IN-The Lyric Theater
12-06	INDIANAPOLIS, IN-The Lyric Theater
12-07	INDIANAPOLIS, IN-The Lyric Theater
12-08	LOUISVILLE, KY-The Rialto Theater for Philip Morris
12-09	SWILTON, AR-High School Auditorium
	and Bob King's Nightclub
12-10	SHREVEPORT, LA-The Louisiana Hayride
12-12	AMORY, MS-The Armory
12-17	SHREVEPORT, LA-The Louisiana Hayride
12-31	SHREVEPORT, LA-The Louisiana Hayride

Concert Log

Showdates 1956

01-01	ST. LOUIS, MO- Kiel Auditorium
01-02	CHARLESTON, MS - High School Auditorium
01-03	BOONEVILLE, MS- Von Theater
01-04	JONESBORO, AR-The Community Center
01-06	RANDOLPH, MS- Hi School
01-07	SHREVEPORT, LA-The Louisiana Hayride
01-14	SHREVEPORT, LA-The Louisiana Hayride
01-15	SAN ANTONIO, TX-Municipal Auditorium
01-16	GALVESTON, TX-City Auditorium
01-17	BEAUMONT, TX-City Auditorium
01-18	AUSTIN, TX-Coliseum
01-19	WICHITA FALLS, TX-Memorial Auditorium
01-20	FORT WORTH, TX-North Side Coliseum
01-21	SHREVEPORT, LA-The Louisiana Hayride
02-05	RICHMOND, VA-Mosque Theater
02-06	GREENSBORO, NC-National Theater
02-07	HIGH POINT, NC-Center
02-08	RALEIGH, NC-Ambassad
02-09	SPARTANBURG, SC-Carolina Theater
02-10	CHARLOTTE, NC-Carolina Theater
02-12	NORFOLK, VA-Municipal Auditorium
02-13	NEWPORT NEWS, VA-Paramount Theater
02-14	WILSON, NC-Charles L. Coon Auditorium
02-15	BURLINGTON, NC-W. Willams High School Auditorium
02-16	WINSTON-SALEM, NC-Carolina Theater
02-19	TAMPA, FL-Ft. Homer Hesterly Armory
02-20	WEST PALM BEACH, FL-Palms Theater
02-21	SARASOTA, FL-Florida Theater
02-22	WAYCROSS, GA-City Auditorium
02-23	JACKSONVILLE, FL-Ball Park
02-24	JACKSONVILLE, FL-Ball Park
02-25	SHREVEPORT, LA-The Louisiana Hayride
02-26	PENSACOLA, FL-City Auditorium
03-03	SHREVEPORT, LA-The Louisiana Hayride
03-09	MEMPHIS, TN-Chisca Hotel
03-10	SHREVEPORT, LA-The Municipal Auditorium
03-14	ATLANTA, GA-Fox Theater
03-15	ATLANTA, GA-Fox Theater
03-18	CHARLESTON, SC-County Hall
03-19	COLUMBIA, SC-Township Auditorium
03-20	AUGUSTA, GA-Bell Municipal Auditorium
03-21	LEXINGTON, NC-YMCA
03-22	RICHMOND, VA-Mosque Theater
03-23	WASHINGTON, DC-S.S. Mount Vernon
03-31	SHREVEPORT, LA-The Louisiana Hayride
04-04	SAN DIEGO, CA-Arena
04-05	SAN DIEGO, CA-Arena

04-08	DENVER, CO-Coliseum
04-09	WICHITA FALLS, TX-Municipal Auditorium
04-10	LUBBOCK, TX-Fair Park Auditorium
04-11	EL PASO, TX-Coliseum
04-12	ALBUQUERQUE, NM-Armory
04-13	AMARILLO, TX-City Auditorium
04-15	SAN ANTONIO, TX-Municipal Auditorium
04-16	CORPUS CHRISTI, TX-Memorial Coliseum
04-17	WACO, TX-Heart O' Texas Coliseum
04-18	TULSA, OK-Fairground Pavillion
04-19	OKLAHOMA CITY, OK-Municipal Auditorium
04-20	FT. WORTH, TX-North Side Coliseum
04-21	HOUSTON, TX-Auditorium
04-23	LAS VEGAS, NV-New Frontier Hotel
	thru 05-06
05-13	ST. PAUL, MN-Auditorium
05-13	MINNEAPOLIS, MN-Auditorium
05-14	LA CROSSE, WI-Mary E. Sawyer Auditorium
05-15	MEMPHIS, TN-The Cotton Festival - Ellis Auditorium
05-16	LITTLE ROCK, AR-Robinson Auditorium
05-17	SPRINGFIELD, MO-Shrine Mosque
05-18	WICHITA, KS-Forum
05-19	LINCOLN, NE-University Of Nebraska Coliseum
05-20	OMAHA, NE-Civic Auditorium
05-21	TOPEKA, KS-Municipal Auditorium
05-22	DES MOINES, IA-Veterans Memorial Auditorium
05-23	SIOUX CITY, IA-City Auditorium
05-24	KANSAS CITY, MO-Municipal Auditorium Arena
05-25	DETROIT, MI-Fox Theater
05-26	COLUMBUS, OH-Veterans Memorial Auditorium
05-27	DAYTON, OH-University Of Dayton Fieldhouse
06-03	OAKLAND, CA-Auditorium Arena
06-06	SAN DIEGO, CA-Arena
06-07	LONG BEACH, CA-Municipal Auditorium
06-08	LOS ANGELES, CA-Shrine Auditorium
06-09	PHOENIX, AZ-State Fairgrounds Grandstand
06-10	TUCSON, AZ-Rodeo Grounds
06-22	ATLANTA, GA-Paramount Theater
06-23	ATLANTA, GA-Paramount Theater
06-24	ATLANTA, GA-Paramount Theater
06-25	SAVANNAH, GA-Sports Arena
06-26	CHARLOTTE, NC-Coliseum
06-27	AUGUSTA, GA-Bell Memorial Auditorium
06-28	CHARLESTON, SC-College Park
06-30	RICHMOND, VA-Shrine Mosque Theater
07-04	MEMPHIS, TN-Russwood Park
08-03	MIAMI, FL-Olympic Theater
08-04	MIAMI, FL-Olympic Theater

08-05	TAMPA, FL-Homer Hesterly Auditorium
08-06	LAKELAND, FL-Polk Theater
08-07	ST. PETERSBURG, FL-Floridian Theater
08-08	ORLANDO, FL-Municipal Auditorium
08-09	DAYTONA BEACH, FL-Peabody Auditorium
08-10	JACKSONVILLE, FL-Florida Theater
08-11	JACKSONVILLE, FL-Florida Theater
08-12	NEW ORLEANS, LA-Municipal Auditorium
09-26	TUPELO, MS-Tupelo Fair Grounds
10-11	DALLAS, TX-Cotton Bowl Stadium
10-12	WACO, TX-Heart O' Texas Coliseum
10-13	HOUSTON, TX-Sam Houston Coliseum
10-14	SAN ANTONIO, TX-Bexar County Coliseum
11-22	TOLEDO, OH-Sports Arena
11-23	CLEVELAND, OH-Arena
11-24	TROY, OH-Hobart Arena
11-25	LOUISVILLE, KY-Jefferson County Armory
12-15	SHREVEPORT, LA-Fair Grounds Youth Center

Showdates 1957

03-28	CHICAGO, IL -International Amphitheatre.
03-29	ST LOUIS, MI -Kiel Auditorium
03-30	FORT WAYNE, IN -Memorial Coliseum
03-31	DETROIT, MI -Olympia Stadium
04-01	BUFFALO, N.Y. -Memorial Auditoirum
04-02	TORONTO, CANADA -Maple Leaf Garden
04-03	OTTOWA, CANADA -Auditorium
04-05	PHILADELPHIA, PA -Arena
04-06	PHILADELPHIA, PA -Arena
08-30	SPOKANE, WA -Memorial Coliseum
08-31	VANCOUVER, CANADA -Empire Stadium
09-01	TACOMA, WA -Lincoln Bowl
	SEATTLE, WA -Sick's Stadium
09-02	PORTLAND, OR-Multnomah Stadium
09-27	TUPELO, MS -Mississippi Alabama Fair & Dairy Show
10-26	SAN FRANCISCO, CA-Civic Auditorium
10-27	OAKLAND, CA-Oakland Auditorium
10-28	LOS ANGELES, CA -Pan Pacific Auditorium
10-29	LOS ANGELES, CA -Pan Pacific Auditorium
11-10	HONOLULU, HA-Honolulu Stadium
11-11	PEARL HARBOUR, HA -Schofield Barracks

Showdates 1961

02-25	MEMPHIS, TN -Ellis Auditorium
03-25	HONOLULU, HA -Bloch Arena

Showdates 1969

07-31	LAS VEGAS, NV. - The International Hotel thru 08-28

Showdates 1970

01-26	LAS VEGAS, NV -The International Hotel thru 02-23
02-27	HOUSTON, TX -The Astrodome
02-28	HOUSTON, TX -The Astrodome
03-01	HOUSTON, TX -The Astrodome
08-10	LAS VEGAS, NV -The International Hotel thru 09-07
09-09	PHOENIX, AZ -Veteran Memorial Coliseum
09-10	ST. LOUIS, MO -Kiel Auditorium
09-11	DETROIT, MI -Olympia
09-12	MIAMI, FL -Convention Center
09-13	TAMPA, FL -Curtis Hixon Hall
09-14	MOBILE, AL -Municipal Auditorium
11-10	OAKLAND, CA -Coliseum
11-11	PORTLAND, OR -Memorial Coliseum
11-12	SEATTLE, WA, -Coliseum
11-13	SAN FRANCISCO, CA-Cow Palace
11-14	LOS ANGELES, CA-Inglewood Forum
11-15	SAN DIEGO, CA -Sports Arena
11-16	OKLAHOMA CITY, OK-Fair Grounds Arena
11-17	DENVER, CO-Denver Coliseum

Showdates 1971

01-26	LAS VEGAS, NV-The International Hotel thru 02-23
07-20	LAKE TAHOE, NV-Sahara Tahoe Hotel thru 08-02
08-09	LAS VEGAS, NV-The Hilton thru 09-06
11-05	MINNEAPOLIS, MI-Metropolitan Sports Arena
11-06	CLEVELAND, OH-Public Hall
11-07	LOUISVILLE, KY-Freedom Hall
11-08	PHILADELPHIA, PA-Spectrum
11-09	BALTIMORE, MD-Civic Center
11-10	BOSTON, MA -Boston Gardens
11-11	CINCINATTI, OH-Cincinatti Gardens
12-12	HOUSTON, TX-Hofheinz Pavillion
12-13	DALLAS, TX-Memorial Auditorium
12-14	TUSCALOOSA, AL-University
12-15	KANSAS CITY, MO-Municipal Auditorium
12-16	SALT LAKE CITY, UT-Salt Palace

Showdates 1972

01-26	LAS VEGAS, NV-The Hilton thru 02-23
04-05	BUFFALO, NY-Memorial Auditorium
04-06	DETROIT, MI-Olympia Stadium
04-07	DAYTON, OH-University Arena
04-08	KNOXVILLE, TN-Stokely Athletics Center
04-09	HAMTON ROADS, VA-Coliseum
04-10	RICHMOND, VA-Coliseum
04-11	ROANOKE, VA-Civic Center
04-12	INDIANAPOLIS, IN-Fair Grounds Coliseum
04-13	CHARLOTTE, NC-Coliseum
04-14	GREENSBORO, NC-Coliseum
04-15	MACON, GA-Coliseum
04-16	JACKSONVILLE, FL-Veteran's Memorial Coliseum
04-17	LITTLE ROCK, AR-T.H. Barton Coliseum
04-18	SAN ANTONIO, TX-Convention Center
04-19	ALDUQUERQUE, NM-Tingley Coliseum
06-09	NEW YORK, NY-Madison Square Garden
06-10	NEW YORK, NY-Madison Square Garden
06-11	NEW YORK, NY-Madison Square Garden
06-12	FORT WAYNE, IN-Memorial Coliseum
06-13	EVANSVILLE, IN-Robert's Municipal Stadium
06-14	MILWAUKEE, WI-Auditorium Arena
06-15	MILWAUKEE, WI-Auditorium Arena
06-16	CHICAGO, IL-Chicago Stadium
06-17	CHICAGO, IL-Chicago Stadium
06-18	FORT WORTH, TX-Tarrant County Convention Center
06-19	WICHITA, KS -Henry Levitt Arena
06-20	TULSA, OK -Civic Assembly Center
08-04	LAS VEGAS, NV-The Hilton thru 09-04
11-08	LUBBOCK, TX-Municipal Coliseum
11-09	TUCSON, AZ-Community Center Arena
11-10	EL PASO, TX-Coliseum
11-11	OAKLAND, CA-Coliseum
11-12	SAN BERNADINO, CA-Swing Auditorium
11-13	SAN BERNADINO, CA-Swing Auditorium
11-14	LONG BEACH, CA-Long Beach Arena
11-15	LONG BEACH, CA-Long Beach Arena
11-17	HONOLULU, HA-The H.I.C. Arena
11-18	HONOLULU, HA-The H.I.C. Arena

Showdates 1973

01-12	HONOLULU, HA-The H.I.C. Arena
01-14	HONOLULU, HA-The H.I.C. Arena
01-26	LAS VEGAS, NV-The Hiltonthru 02-23
04-22	PHOENIX, AZ-Veterans Memorial Coliseum
04-23	ANAHEIM, CA-Convention Center
04-24	ANAHEIM, CA-Convention Center
04-25	FRESNO, CA-Selland Arena
04-26	SAN DIEGO, CA-Sports Arena
04-27	PORTLAND, OR-Coliseum
04-28	SPOKANE, WA-Coliseum
04-29	SEATTLE, WA-Center Arena
04-30	DENVER, CO-Denver Coliseum
05-04	LAKE TAHOE, NV-Sahara Tahoe Hotel thru 05-16
06-20	MOBILE, AL -Municipal Auditorium
06-21	ATLANTA, GA-Omni Coliseum
06-22	UNIONDALE, NY-Nassau Veteran Memorial Coliseum
06-23	UNIONDALE, NY-Nassau Veteran Memorial Coliseum
06-24	UNIONDALE, NY-Nassau Veteran Memorial Coliseum
06-25	PITTSBURG, PA-Civic Center Arena
06-26	PITTSBURG, PA-Civic Center Arena
06-27	CINCINATTI, OH-Cincinatti Gardens
06-28	ST. LOUIS, MO-Kiel Auditorium
06-29	ATLANTA, GA-Omni Coliseum
06-30	ATLANTA, GA-Omni Coliseum
07-01	NASHVILLE, TN-Municipal Auditorium
07-02	OKLAHOMA CITY, OK-Myriad Center Arena
07-03	ATLANTA, GA Omni Coliseum
08-06	LAS VEGAS, NV-The Hilton thru 09-03

Showdates 1974

01-26	LAS VEGAS, NV-The Hilton /thru 02-09
03-01	TULSA, OK-Oral Roberts University. Mabee Center
03-02	TULSA, OK-Oral Roberts University. Mabee Center
03-03	HOUSTON, TX-The Atrodome
03-04	MONROE, LA-The Astrodome
03-05	AUBURN, AL-University
03-06	MONTGOMERY,A - Garrett Coliseum
03-07	MONROE, LA-Civic Center
03-08	MONROE, LA-Civic Center
03-09	CHARLOTTE, NC-Coliseum
03-10	ROANOKE, VA-Civic Center
03-11	HAMPTON, VA-Hampton Roads Coliseum
03-12	RICHMOND, VA-Coliseum
03-13	GREENSBORO, NC-Coliseum
03-14	MURFREESBORO, TN-Middle Tennessee State University
03-15	KNOXVILLE, TN-University Of Tennessee

Concert Log

03-16	MEMPHIS, TN-Mid-South Coliseum					

08-02	ROANOKE, VA-Civic Center	
08-03	FAYETTEVILLE, NC-Cumberland County Memorial Auditorium	
08-04	FAYETTEVILLE, NC-Cumberland County Memorial Auditorium	
08-05	FAYETTEVILLE, NC-Cumberland County Memorial Auditorium	
08-27	SAN ANTONIO, TX-Convention Center	
08-28	HOUSTON, TX-The Summit	
08-29	MOBILE, AL-Municipal Auditorium	
08-30	TUSCALOOSA, AL-University Of Alabama	
08-31	MACON, GA-Coliseum	
09-01	JACKSONVILLE, FL-Coliseum	
09-02	TAMPA, FL-Curtis Hixon Hall	
09-03	ST. PETERSBURG, FL-Bay Front Center	
09-04	LAKELAND, FL-Civic Center	
09-05	JACKSON, MS-State Fair Civic Center	
09-06	HUNTSVILLE, AL-Von Braun Civic Center	
09-07	PINE BLUFF, AR-Convention Center	
09-08	PINE BLUFF, AR-Convention Center	
10-14	CHICAGO, IL-Chicago Stadium	
10-15	CHICAGO, IL-Chicago Stadium	
10-16	DULUTH, MN-Arena	
10-17	BLOOMINGTON, MN-Metropolitan Sports Center	
10-18	SIOUX FALLS, SD-Arena	
10-19	MADISON, WI-Dane County Coliseum	
10-20	NOTRE DAME, IN-University	
10-21	KALAMAZOO, MI-Wings Stadium	
10-22	CHAMPAIGN, IL-University	
10-23	RICHFIELD, OH-Coliseum	
10-24	EVANSVILLE, IN-Roberts Stadium	
10-25	FORT WAYNE, IN-Memorial Coliseum	
10-26	DAYTON, OH-University	
10-27	CARBONDALE, IL-Southern Illinois University	
11-24	RENO, NV-Sparks Convention Center	
11-25	EUGENE, OR-MacArthur Court	
11-26	PORTLAND, OR-Memorial Coliseum	
11-27	EUGENE, OR-MacArthur Court	
11-28	SAN FRANCISCO, CA-Cow Palace	
11-29	SAN FRANCISCO, CA-Cow Palace	
11-30	ANAHEIM, CA-Convention Center	
12-02	LAS VEGAS, NV-The Hilton thru 12-12	
12-27	WICHITA, KS-State University	
12-28	DALLAS, TX-Memorial Auditorium	
12-29	BIRMINGHAM, AL-Jefferson Coliseum	
12-30	ATLANTA, GA-Omni Coliseum	
12-31	PITTSBURGH, PA-Civic Center Arena	

Showdates – 1977

02-12	MIAMI, FL-Sportatorium
02-13	W. PALM BEACH, FL-Auditorium
02-14	ST. PETERSBURG, FL-Bay Front Center
02-15	ORLANDO, FL-Sports Stadium
02-16	MONTGOMERY, AL-Garret Coliseum
02-17	SAVANNAH, GA-Civic Center
02-18	COLUMBIA, SC-Coliseum
02-19	JOHNSON CITY, TN-Freedom Hall
02-20	CHARLOTTE, NC-Coliseum
02-21	CHARLOTTE, NC-Coliseum
03-23	TEMPE, AZ-Arizona State University
03-24	AMARILLO, TX-Civic Center
03-25	NORMAN, OK-University Of Oklahoma
03-26	NORMAN, OK-University Of Oklahoma
03-27	ABILENE, TX-Taylor County Coliseum
03-28	AUSTIN, TX-Municipal Auditorium
03-29	ALEXANDRIA, LA-Rapides Parish Coliseum
03-30	ALEXANDRIA, LA-Rapides Parish Coliseum
04-21	GREENSBORO, NC-Coliseum
04-22	DETROIT, MI-Olympia Stadium
04-23	TOLEDO, OH-University
04-24	ANN ARBOR, MI-Crisler Arena
04-25	SAGINAW, MI-Center
04-26	KALAMAZOO, MI-Wings Stadium
04-27	MILWAUKEE, WI-Arena
04-28	GREEN BAY, WI-Veteran's Memorial Coliseum
04-29	DULUTH, MN-Arena
04-30	ST. PAUL, MN-Civic Center
05-01	CHICAGO, IL-Stadium
05-02	CHICAGO, IL-Stadium
05-03	SAGINAW, MI-Center
05-20	KNOXVILLE, TN-University Of Tennessee
05-21	LOUISVILLE, KY-Freedom Hall
05-22	LANDOVER, MD-Capital Center
05-23	PROVIDENCE, RI-Civic Center
05-24	AUGUSTA, ME-Civic Center
05-25	ROCHESTER, NY-Community War Memorial
05-26	BINGHAMPTON, NY -
05-27	BINGHAMPTON, NY -
05-28	PHILADELPHIA, PA-The Spectrum
05-29	BALTIMORE, MD-Civic Center
05-30	JACKSONVILLE, FL-Coliseum
05-31	BATON ROUGE, LA-Louisiana State University
06-01	MACON, GA-Coliseum
06-02	MOBILE, AL-Municipal Auditorium
06-17	SPRINGFEILD, MO-South West Missouri State University

06-18	KANSAS CITY, MO-Kemper Arena
06-19	OMAHA, NE-City Auditorium Arena
06-20	LINCOLN, NE-Pershin Municipal Auditorium
06-21	RAPID CITY, SD-Mount Rusmore Civic Center
06-22	SIOUX FALLS, SD-Arena
06-23	DES MOINES, IA-Veteran's Memorial Coliseum
06-24	MADISON, WI-Dane County Coliseum
06-25	CINCINATTI, OH-River Front Coliseum
06-26	INDIANAPOLIS, IN-Market Square Arena

Information compiled by Ernst Mikael Jørgensen.
Copyright 1995. It's Magic-Katrinebjerg 10,
D.K. 4440 Denmark.

Thanks to Peter Guralnick, Brian Petersen,
Sean O'Neal, Lee Cotton, Peter Schittler, Shelley Ritter
and Stein Erik Skar.

Acknowledgements

The Publishers would like to thank the management and staff at Elvis Presley Enterprises for their assistance in making this book possible, with special thanks to:

Todd Morgan – Creative Resources Director
Pete Davidson – Senior Licensing Manager
Danna Yarmowich – Licensing Manager

The author would like to thank Shelley Ritter, Greg Howell, Liz Awsumb, Betina Ong, Rosalind McDermott, Todd Morgan, Bridgette Cleaves, Peter Guralnick and *Last Train To Memphis*, my agents Dick McDonough and Tina Betts, Mike Evans, and my wife Tara McAdams.

This book is dedicated to Scotty Moore and D.J.Fontana

Picture Acknowledgements:

Memorabilia photography and special photographic services by **Gil Michael Photography, Memphis**.

The Publishers would like to thank all those who have supplied photographic material for use in this book and apologize to any whose contribution may have been inadvertently omitted from these acknowledgements.

All archival photographs are from the collection of **Elvis Presley Enterprises, Inc.,** except for the following:
Archive Photos /Alpha Blair 194 left, 194 bottom, 194 top
Hulton Deutsch Collection 42 /43
Range Pictures Ltd /UPI Photo 166 left, 166 right
Joseph A. Tunzi 180 left, 180 right, 181, 183, 193
Alfred Wertheimer 46, 47, 52 /53, 62, 63, 64/65, 70
Bob Williams 48/49

OTTAWA CITIZEN

OTTAWA, CANADA, WEDNESDAY, APRIL 3, 1957

Labor Day Really

Elvis Arrives Here in Person

THE OREGONIAN, TUESDAY, SEPTEMBER 3, 1957

...K UP This is what some 14,600 real ...mah st...
...gone Presley fans saw at Multno- to reli...